REPORTING BACK

Memories of a Lifetime

Tony Pyatt

First Edition produced in association with
Bound Biographies
Boundary House, 23 Thompson Drive
Bicester, Oxon OX27 8FA

Second Edition
Blaisdon Publishing
3 Park Chase, Hornby, Bedale
North Yorkshire DL8 1PR
www.blaisdon.force9.co.uk

ISBN 1 90283831 9

Cover: *The colours are those of the Royal Tank Regiment,*
signifying: "Through mud and through blood to
the green fields beyond."

Dedication

To my wife Audrey
(1922-2000)

and to my children and grandchildren

As We Were in 1939

Tony at 22

Audrey at 17

Contents

Illustrations

Author's Note

It is likely that this book would not have been written but for the expressed determination of my two daughters that I should set down as much as I could remember about my life, in the interest of all my children and extended family.

This I have tried to do, the result being, I hope, that my story will be of interest not only to them but also to members of our wider family circle and my many friends. It has been hand-written over a period of about two-and-a-half years – at home in Waldringfield, at Elizabeth's in Norway, Vivienne's in Cape Town, and at Stephen's in Warwickshire – and typed at home.

In the course of writing this book I may have made a few mistakes over dates or the sequence of events, and if I have omitted to mention some relatives, friends or colleagues then I ask for my readers' forgiveness and indulgence – and put such errors and omissions down to my advancing years. Happy reading!

Tony Pyatt
September 2003

Early Childhood

1916-1920

I was a war baby – a Great War baby – born on 23rd September 1916 halfway through the terrible conflict of 1914-18. And it was appropriate, as will be appreciated later in this book, that I should have arrived on the scene just eight days after tanks, invented by the British, had gone into action on a large scale for the very first time – to the amazement and consternation of the Germans on the Western Front.

I was born in the little Kent village of Oare, near Faversham, which makes me, I believe, a Man of Kent rather than a Kentish Man had I been delivered on the other side of the River Medway. It could be said that my birthplace was chosen for me by the Army, for at the time my father, Percival Henry, was an officer in the Royal Artillery stationed nearby, and he and my mother, Evelyn Vernon, 'lived out' in the area. I was christened Anthony Henry.

In the days leading up to the war my father's parents, Henry and Clara Pyatt, were living at Esher in Surrey. My father was an only child and in civilian life he was a commercial traveller.

My grandfather was the London manager of a Swiss firm, *Zaehner & Schiess & Co.*, manufacturers of organdie, a material then used in dressmaking. My grandmother interested herself in the Sunshine Guild, a charity which helped poor children in London.

Behind my grandparents' house were tennis courts and it was on these courts that my father, then aged about 24, met the girl who was to become his wife and my mother – Evelyn Vernon McGarey. She was 26 and the youngest of the five surviving children of Thomas McGarey, who had died in 1892, and of Evelyn Margaret McGarey, who was living in the Twickenham area.

Father and Mother in an Army car during the First World War

My mother had two brothers, Thomas William (Willie) and Charles Graham, and two sisters, Edith Graham (Edie) and Marion Jane Ashley – all McGareys, of course.

I have the McGarey family tree going back more than 180 years (at the time of writing) to 1819, and that of the O'Callaghans, my mother's family, to the year 1829. My maternal grandfather came from a Scottish family and became a stationmaster in the South of England; my grandmother's forebears were Irish.

My Uncle Willie never married; neither did either of my two aunts, Edie and Marion. Uncle Graham had two sons, Donald and Vernon, both of whom died in the 1990s, and a daughter, Margaret Alice, who died towards the end of 2001.

My mother and me

With my parents in a cornfield in 1918

On my father's side I had neither uncles and aunts nor cousins, but I did have a number of 'great' relations and I do just remember my Grandma Pyatt's father, my Great-grandpa Musgrave.

The Pyatts could not have lived at Oare for very long because in April 1918 my sister Bunty was born at Redhill, in the adjoining county of Surrey. Her baptismal names are Gladys Evelyn Clara but she has never been known by these. The next move, I believe, was to the Northampton area and, eventually, to Twickenham in Middlesex. The war was nearing its closing stages and my father was in command of an anti-aircraft battery sited on Tower Bridge in London.

At Twickenham we lived beside the Thames. Nearby there was an ammunition factory and one day, I'm told, my mother, busy attending to my baby sister, realised that her two-year-old son was missing. After a frantic search I was discovered at the factory having wandered off to see what was going on there and was fortunately returned to my anxious parent.

Three other incidents about this time go to show what a handful of a toddler I was. The first was another disappearing act – I was found in an empty dustbin with the lid on! The second incident could have had more serious consequences. I moved a metal 'slop-pail' from outside a bedroom to the top of the stairs, with the result that my mother tripped over it when carrying the baby, the contents of the pail streaming over the landing carpet and down the stairs. Finally, (for the time being) I pushed the pram in which Bunty was sleeping, tipped it up and deposited Bunty on the ground – with a broken arm. This was not the proudest period of my life!

With the coming of the year 1919 a vicious 'flu epidemic spread across Europe and beyond. Millions of people died world-wide. My mother may have caught the virus – I cannot be sure about this – but I do know that in November of that year she was taken ill with pleurisy and it was this that led to her death at the age of 30.

My father (seated on the left) with a group of fellow officers during the First World War

My mother

Had there been antibiotics in those days she might well have survived the illness. I was then 3 years old and Bunty was only 18 months – both of us, unfortunately, too young to have any memory of her. For me this has always been a matter of extreme regret and sorrow. My mother was a beautiful woman with a sweet nature – that much I have been able to glean over the years. She is buried alongside her mother in the family grave in Twickenham cemetery.

Her premature death just a year after the war ended left my father with the problem of looking after two very young children. He obviously needed help and this came from two quarters, my father's parents at Esher and my mother's two unmarried sisters, Edie and Marion, the former becoming in effect a housekeeper and nanny.

For a time Bunty and I would be in a rented house with our Auntie Edie while my father – by now out of the Army, of course – carried on with his job as a commercial traveller, visiting various towns in East Anglia and elsewhere in the Eastern Counties by train. His merchandise was women's dresses and underwear – later his range extended to silk stockings and swimwear – and today he would be called a 'rep'. In the larger towns such as Norwich, Ipswich and Cambridge he rented stock rooms where his range of clothing was inspected by staff from the local retail shops. One of these stock rooms, now used for quite a different purpose, still exists behind what used to be the *Crown and Anchor Hotel* in Ipswich and is today the *W.H. Smith* shop. My father's clothing samples were moved around the country in large boxes known as skips.

My memories of events between 1919 and the early '20s are, of course, faint – I was only 3 or 4 years old – but even today I can recall odd moments. For instance, in my mind I can still see the steps leading up to the front door of the Victorian house in Hampstead where we lived with Auntie Edie, and in the hall a model airplane suspended from the ceiling by thin wires. I remember one Christmas with my grandparents at Esher, either in 1919 or 1920, when my father dressed up as Santa Claus. I can almost feel the thrill I experienced when he knocked on the door and entered bearing a sackful of presents. I think Bunty was still far too young then for her to have any memory of that occasion.

At first my grandmother had a live-in maid, and later a succession of daily maids – she was so fussy that none would stay in her service for very long! My grandfather travelled by train to the City every weekday – and continued to do so for over fifty years.

About this time, when I was no more than 4, I went to my first school. This was held in a private house in Esher and each day a little girl – presumably she was considered to be old enough to be out on her own – called to take me there and bring me home. I remember that we always stopped at a small hut, or kiosk, on the way to buy a penny bar of toffee. I recall, too, being taught to write by joining up a series of dots which formed the letters of the alphabet.

During the summer of 1920 my father rented a picturesque cottage on the Isle of Wight. There, with Auntie Edie and a temporary nanny employed to help her, Bunty and I spent happy days playing on the beach nearby. Holidaymakers would always be interested in the very tiny church (still there, of course) which was a feature of the village, but I imagine they must have been somewhat taken aback when they often found their guide was a precocious little boy!

My father managed to spend a week or two with us, and one day when a rail strike was in progress and no trains were running, he took me on to the railway line which ran close to the cottage and we walked a few yards into a long tunnel cut through the surrounding hill.

My father and Bunty in 1920, and Bunty on honeymoon, 1940,
outside the cottage at St Lawrence

Seventy years later, during an Isle of Wight holiday, I walked further into this same tunnel – no railway lines now, just mushrooms being grown commercially and the far end blocked off.

Just one other lingering memory of our stay on the Isle of Wight: our journeys to and from the railway station were in a pony and trap, and after partly eating an apple it started to turn brown – I just couldn't understand why!

My father with me and Bunty at Esher in 1922

Schooldays and a New Mother

1920-1932

It must have been towards the end of 1920 or in the early part of 1921 that on his travels in East Anglia my father stayed in Wisbech in Cambridgeshire, meeting friends who introduced him to Gertrude Mary Dockerill – then only 21 or 22 – the girl who was to become his second wife and my step-mother. At that time she was working as a cashier in a local grocery shop. Her meeting with my father probably took place in a popular Wisbech hostelry, the *Spread Eagle*, where she and her particular girl friends, 'Flap' and Mabel, were acquainted with the landlord's family.

Bunty and I were then with either our grandparents or Auntie Edie, but it was not long before I was taken to Wisbech to meet the lady who, initially, was to be my 'Auntie Gertie'. She made a great fuss of me and we soon established a very happy relationship which was to last for nearly 60 years until her death in 1979. I feel sure that Bunty was not with me at that particular time – probably my father considered it would be more expedient for his future wife to be introduced in stages to the young family she was going to inherit.

At any rate, I recall becoming a frequent visitor to what for me was quite another world. My father's parents were typical middle-class people of the time, living in some style and with very definite ideas about the way children should be brought up and to what they should, or should not, be exposed. It must, therefore, have been an eye-opener to me to be introduced to a much more relaxed atmosphere in very different surroundings.

My new grandmother-to-be, Grannie Dockerill, was a very loving and kindly person, the widow of a police constable who had died of pneumonia in his forties after nights on the beat in bad weather. She lived in a very small terraced house and took in lodgers to make ends meet. 'Auntie Gertie' lived there, too, but her two brothers, Arthur and Sidney, were away from home, Arthur serving in the Royal Marines and travelling the world in battleships and Sidney in the Army in India.

On my visits to Wisbech, when I was aged between 5 and 6, I soon became an enthusiastic film fan. 'Auntie Gertie' used to take me to the *Hippodrome*, where silent films were shown and stage 'turns' were included in the evening's programme. The films were always accompanied by a pianist – sometimes even by a small orchestra – who played music appropriate to what was being shown on the screen. This was the normal procedure in all cinemas at the time, though some of the larger ones had Wurlitzer organs. 'Talkies' did not arrive on the scene until 1928-30.

I was particularly thrilled by the serials when, for example, the heroine was seen tied to a railway line by the villain as an express train approached, or to a tree in the jungle as a lion leapt towards her, and the caption on the screen proclaimed, "Will Mary survive? See next week's thrilling instalment." These were indeed exciting times for a 5-year-old, especially one who had hitherto been 'protected' from the wicked world.

In December 1922 my father and 'Auntie Gertie', then 23, married in a quiet ceremony at St Augustine's Church, Wisbech, marking the start of a new family life for Bunty and me. Bunty, I think, was not present but in Auntie Edie's care. I have to confess that, no doubt to everyone's embarrassment, I really did make my presence felt, for at the reception at the house of an aunt of my new mother I created a fuss when the happy couple were about to leave for their honeymoon in Manchester and refused to be left behind. So with them I went! Just how my mother felt about this I don't know, but as I had become very attached to my father he may not have been entirely surprised by my behaviour.

At 5 ½ years old...and at Cliftonville in 1923

Our first home as a new family was in a house at New Malden in Surrey where, just down the road in the main street, my Auntie Edie had a small baby-clothing shop. Before long we moved to Richmond, where I was sent to a small private school to resume my interrupted education, and it was while we were there that I was taken to the great British Empire Exhibition at Wembley when the new stadium was opened (rather more successful than the Dome). At the FA Cup Final on 28 April 1923, the first to be played there, the crowd numbered 126,000 and 75,000 more got in free by scrambling over the stadium wall! Thousands spilled on to the pitch, which had to be cleared by mounted police. The match resulted in a 2-1 win for Bolton Wanderers over West Ham.

Crowds spill onto the pitch at the first Wembley Cup Final in 1923

The great exhibition itself attracted many thousands of people. It combined a variety of amusements with what could be described as a showcase of industrial and technological achievements of the day. I can still picture in my mind a very smart *Model-T Ford* equipped as a taxi. Five days earlier when the reigning monarch, King George V, opened the Exhibition, he sent a telegram to himself routed from London to London via the British Empire. The telegraphic message passed through Canada, New Zealand, Australia, South Africa, India, Aden, Egypt and Gibraltar in one minute 20 seconds before being returned to the King 'in good order' by a young telegraph boy before an assembly of 50,000 people – quite an achievement in those days.

Another treat for us at this time was the Lord Mayor's Show in the City of London. Bunty and I were taken up to the City by our grandmother, and as our grandfather's offices were in the heart of the business quarter we had a grandstand view of the show from an upper window. I was reminded of the several times we watched this annual procession through the City when I switched on the television in November 2000 and saw the latest and most impressive Lord Mayor's Show – after a gap of well over 70 years.

Our home in Rosemont Road, Richmond, was not far from Richmond Park, where the Duke and Duchess of York – later King George VI and Queen Elizabeth – lived in a royal house. Also in the immediate area, at the top of Richmond Hill overlooking the Thames, stood a very large new building, the Star and Garter Home, built to house and care for military victims of the Great War so recently ended. It is still there today, though now it also accommodates severely disabled civilians with military connections (perhaps, through a father or brother) who need constant care. One of the patients there today is the daughter of my late cousin Vernon who died in the '90s. A victim of severe multiple sclerosis, she has been in the home for many years.

One of our neighbours in Rosemont Road was a man whose hobby centred on the latest of inventions at that time – the wireless. He had a large set with many valves. These were the forerunners of transistors and sat in a row on the outside of the set. To change wavelengths, from long to medium or short, one had to pull out a large 'coil' and insert another one – a far cry from the radios of today! Around this time, too, I had been taken by my Aunt Edie to the Hertfordshire farm of a friend who owned a 'crystal set'; such radios require neither mains power nor batteries and I spent happy hours 'tickling' the crystal to get a response from the *BBC*, whose broadcasting to the nation had started only a couple of years earlier in 1922. Years later, as a father, I constructed a crystal set for my young sons.

* * * * *

It was while we were living in Richmond that my stepmother, now more familiarly called Mum, was taken ill. I was far too young to be told what was wrong but I have no doubt now that she suffered a miscarriage. At any rate, I was packed off to Wisbech to live for about a year with Grannie Dockerill as it was evidently considered that having Bunty at home was quite enough for Mum to look after.

There were very limited facilities in Grannie's small house – no bathroom (only hand washbasins and water jugs in the bedrooms), an outside lavatory without mains water (just a pump in the yard and a bucket), no kitchen sink (a hand bowl instead) and a basic gas stove. The gas supply – downstairs lights only – came via a meter in the living room which had to be fed with pennies! We used candles to provide light in the upstairs rooms.

Between the yard and the small garden was an outhouse where Grannie did the washing in a solid-fuel copper, squeezing out the water between the rollers of a hand-operated mangle.

They were happy days with Grannie Dockerill – instructive ones, too, for she taught me how to spell ("No tea until you've told me how to spell bread") and knocked a lot of snobbishness out of me ("Don't you dare call those children guttersnipes again," she said when I used that description about some very poorly dressed children we passed one day). Yes, I learnt much from Grannie in the year that I lived with her.

I went to a small private school – Miss Charlesworth's – and made new friends. One, strangely enough, was named Friend – his father made a lot of money running a scrap-merchant's business and was also chief of the local (volunteer) fire brigade. On Sunday evenings I sat with my grandmother in a pew at the back of the Parish Church, St Peter's. I'm sure that that set the foundation of the faith which has stood me in good stead over the past eighty years and keeps me going today.

My stepmother with Grannie Dockerill and Una in later years

Grannie Dockerill's house was quite close to a large park, where I spent many happy hours on the swings and see-saw in the children's section. In those days these amusements were padlocked on Sundays – playing wasn't officially allowed on the Sabbath! The one other feature of the park still fresh in my memory – perhaps for obvious reasons in view of my Army days in later years – was a World War I tank displayed in the centre, a stark reminder to everyone of the Great War which had not long ended.

There came the day when I rejoined my parents and Bunty in Richmond, but it was not long before we were on the move again, this time to Berrylands on the outskirts of Surbiton, where we lived in a Victorian house with a basement. Nearly sixty years later my granddaughter Emma went to a private school only a hundred yards or so from the site of our old home, which has now been replaced by a block of flats, and my daughter Vivienne lived in the same area.

At Berrylands I started as a pupil at Arundel House School, Surbiton, and Bunty went to Surbiton College. The boys' school was run by a Mr Bastaple and his wife was head of the girls'.

In next to no time we left Berrylands to move into a modern house in Grove Road, Surbiton, itself. Here my sister Una was born on 11th May 1926, when I was coming up 10 and Bunty was 8½, and for the remainder of our days in Surbiton we continued at our respective schools. An abiding memory of the time is of the General Strike which almost brought the country to a standstill. Not quite though, for bowler-hatted businessmen forsook their offices to take to rail and road, driving trains and buses to keep public transport going. Somehow the country survived and within less than a fortnight life returned to normal.

Two other incidents come to mind. One evening my mother and father left Bunty and me in bed while they visited friends. I'm sure they must have told us not to answer any knocks on the door – but we did, of course. I expect I was the culprit! At any rate, one of us went downstairs in response to a knock, opened the door and was confronted by our Uncle Willie, who had called on the chance of finding *all* the family at home. He was a bit taken back when he found that Bunty and I were on our own, but he read us some stories before departing. I never did find out how explanations were received when contact was later made between my parents and my uncle but I do know that I received a severe ticking off for being disobedient.

On another occasion I took Bunty to the local cinema, the *Coronation* at the bottom of Surbiton Hill, about mid-afternoon and insisted that we stay to see the programme round twice. As a result we arrived home after 8.00 pm. Another (deserved) ticking off!

* * * * *

With the country slowly recovering from the Great War, the '20s were years of high unemployment which continued well into the '30s. They were also years which saw rapid developments in communication – the birth of the *BBC*, for example – and aviation, and the expansion of the motor industry as mass production gave the 'ordinary man' the chance to own a car. There was also the first 'New Look' as women took to wearing short skirts, and hairdressing salons boomed with the introduction of 'permanent waving' and the 'bob' and 'shingle' cuts. In dance halls the *Charleston* was all the rage. On the beaches bathing machines – huts on wheels with steps down to the water which afforded swimmers privacy when they changed into and out of their 'costumes' – were still in evidence, though dwindling in number as 'mixed bathing' became more acceptable.

The bathing party – on the beach at Cliftonville with my stepmother and her friend Mabel in 1925

Great strides were being made in flying, the Atlantic having been crossed by air for the first time in 1919 by the aviators Allcock and Brown. Other flyers whose names were to become famous in the '20s and '30s were making the headlines – people such as Charles Lindbergh, Jim Mollison, Amy Johnson and Amelia Earhart. Motor racing took off: Brooklands race track was constructed, Bentleys reigned supreme and the world land speed record was broken again and again by such British drivers as Sir Malcolm Campbell, in successive Bluebirds, Sir Henry Seagrave, in his Golden Arrow, and Parry Thomas. Early in the '30s when Sir Malcolm took the record to over 246 mph on the salt lake flats in the United States I drew a picture of Bluebird, coloured it and sent it to my hero. Imagine my surprise and great delight when Sir Malcolm returned it to me, autographed, and sent with it a covering letter.

It was in the '20s that trans-Atlantic travel increased in popularity. Ships were then the only means of taking people across the ocean and large liners had been in use for some years – the Titanic, for instance, which went down in 1912 after striking an iceberg, and the Lusitania, sunk during the Great War. Plying the waves now were such famous, luxury liners as the Berengaria and the Mauritania with the two queens, the Queen Mary and the Queen Elizabeth, soon to follow – both, in their day, the largest in the world.

Personal memories of our days in Surbiton are of walks down to the banks of the Thames, going to Sunday school and prizing the biblical stamps that were handed out, making a tent in the garden out of chairs and a blanket, and the gymnasium at school where I showed some prowess on the parallel bars, silent films at the cinema, and the day when a suspected burglar took refuge in our front garden as he was being chased by police. As far as I remember we induced him to give himself up.

Over all these years and subsequently Bunty and I were frequent visitors to our grandparents at Esher, to our aunts and uncle and also to our Grandma McGarey, who lived until 1927.

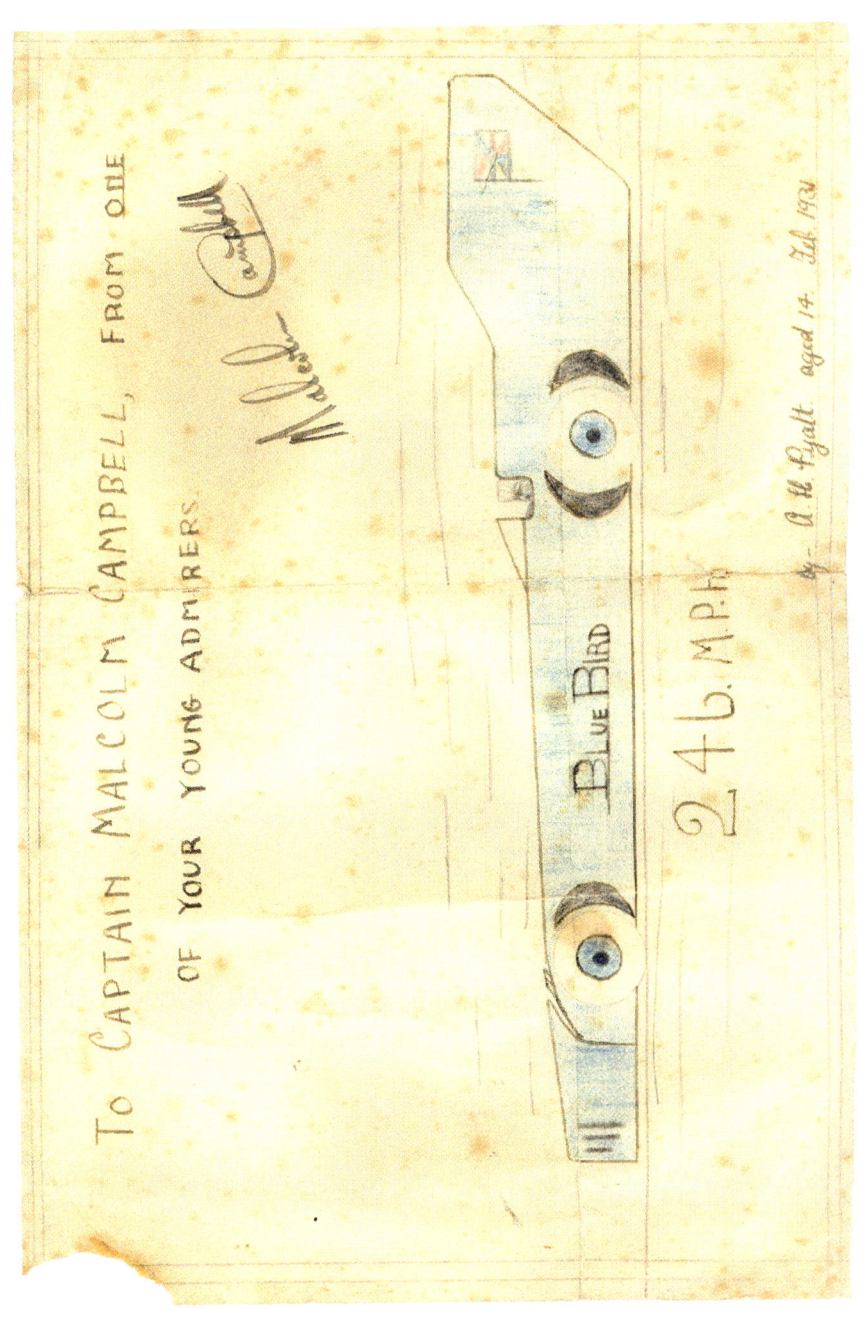

My drawing of Bluebird

OLD BOND STREET HOUSE,

6-8, OLD BOND STREET,

LONDON, W.1.

17th March 1931.

Master A.H.Pyatt,
16 Oakroyd Crescent,
Wisbech.

Dear Pyatt,

Very many thanks for your extremely
good drawing of the Blue Bird which I was
very pleased indeed to receive.

As this must have taken you some time
to do, I thought possibly you might like to
keep it, so I am returning it herewith and
have autographed it for you.

With all best wishes,

Yours sincerely,

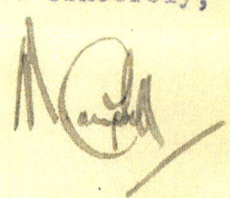

Malcolm Campbell's letter

40

Our grandparents were always very kind and generous in all sorts of ways. We spent holidays with them and later on, when my father's fortunes were waning – as they frequently did – they paid our school fees.

Aunties Edie and Marion were also very good to us, and so was Uncle Willie, who by this time was living in Exeter with Auntie Edie as his housekeeper (after her death in 1938 Auntie Marion replaced her). Separately, Bunty and I spent many summer holidays at their house on Cowick Hill; I would meet Uncle Willie at his office when he finished work for the day and we'd take the train to Dawlish Warren to have a swim.

When I stayed with my grandparents at Esher a close companion was a boy named Raymond Huckle. He and I would go on to the common alongside the main railway line, which in my young days was also one of the local golf courses, and try our hand at the game; not that these early practice efforts did much for the golf which I took up in later years! We also amused ourselves by taking old golf balls to pieces to see what was inside. At other times we would take the train from the nearest railway station, Thames Ditton, to Surbiton and go to the Coronation cinema.

For a while after Una was born my mother employed a live-in 'companion-help' whose job it was to assist in caring for the new baby and generally to ease the burden of housework. She also took Bunty and me on those walks to the river. This young lady had a boy-friend who, to my great interest and excitement, would arrive at our home on a motor-cycle. I think it was a Rudge-Multi, but whatever it was, I was thrilled to be allowed to sit on the pillion seat – whether the machine was in motion or not I cannot recall.

During my years in Surbiton I was a member of the choir of St Mark's Church at the top of the hill between Surbiton and

Berrylands. If I was rather fidgety on cold winter Sundays it was because as a boy I suffered intensely from chilblains on my feet.

* * * * *

In 1927 we said goodbye to Surbiton and moved to Wisbech, making the journey in a friend's car, a *Renault* I believe, which had at that time a peculiarly-shaped bonnet resembling an elephant's trunk. Wisbech was, of course, a more realistic centre from which my father would travel to various parts of East Anglia and beyond in Eastern England.

The first of the five houses we were to live in over the next nine years in the Cambridgeshire town was in Burcroft Road. A semi-detached house, it was much smaller and far less well-appointed than our house in Surbiton. There was gas lighting in the down-stairs rooms only; candles were the order of the day (or, rather, night) upstairs and I cannot remember there being a bathroom. But we had a nice garden, though Dad left most of the work in it to Mum – with some help from me.

One summer during our early days in Wisbech, when Bunty and I were staying alternately in Exeter with Uncle William and Auntie Edie and with our grandparents in Esher, I literally became a 'little boy lost'. It was quite the normal thing in those days to put young children on trains either in charge of the guard or in the care of someone who appeared to be a respectable adult. I had in fact made several journeys in this way when I was as young as 5, once from London to Exeter in the guard's van of the train.

For this latest journey my mother saw me off on my own at the M&GN (Midland & Great Northern) station in Wisbech, happy (or so she thought) in the knowledge that I would be met by my grandfather at King's Cross. Unfortunately, she had forgotten to post the letter giving the day and time of my arrival and it was not until late in the evening that she found the letter in a pocket! By then it was, of course, too late to put things right.

Well, the train duly steamed into King's Cross, I gathered my things, stepped on to the platform and started to look for my grandfather. No grandfather, and to make matters worse I had no money. There was only one thing to do – find a policeman and tell him of my predicament. A very kindly railway policeman came to my rescue. As I knew the name of my grandfather's firm in the City, he was able to make a phone call to report where I was and make arrangements for me to be escorted on the Underground to Waterloo. There I was met by my grandfather and we travelled to Esher.

I think I can honestly say that although I was only about 11 at the time I was not unduly worried by the experience. But, especially in today's climate, I would not recommend it.

When I was 11, I started at Wisbech Grammar School, as a 'paying' pupil, courtesy of my benevolent grandfather, who also paid for Bunty to go to the Convent School. My school was one the oldest in Britain and is still going today. It was founded in 1379 and two years after my arrival we celebrated its 550th anniversary. Fifty years on, in 1979, as an old boy of the school, I attended celebrations to mark the 600th year of its foundation. I had retired the previous year.

I made many new friends at the Grammar School, nearly all of them being much taller than me. One was Eric Nicholas who started on the same day as I did, his family having just moved to the town from London. Our southern accents were regarded with some curiosity if not actual animosity. Eric, whose father was a postman, became an architect. Another boy became a motor engineer, serving an apprenticeship with the then *Austin Motor Company* at Longbridge, Birmingham. While there he acquired a car – a two-seater *Morris Minor* rather than an *Austin 7* as security rules prohibited employees owning vehicles which used *Austin* parts.

Grandpa Pyatt

Grandpa and Grandma Pyatt at Margate in 1924

45

One of the highlights of the year in Wisbech was the Mart, a week-long fair with lots of roundabouts, sideshows and stalls which was held in the main streets and the two market places. Every night the town would be crowded with people, young and old, with organ music blaring out from all sides. Our precious pennies were soon spent, though some of my friends with more affluent parents would have as much as ten shillings (50p) in their pockets – a princely sum then.

Another of my school friends, Tom Walton, also became a journalist – the last I heard of him, many years ago, he was a reporter on the *Worthing Herald* in Sussex. His younger brother was an extremely good swimmer and diver and we gave him the rather uncomplimentary nickname of 'Slimy'.

We all either walked or rode bicycles to school and came home for 'dinner' every day at 12.30 pm. Dinners at school were provided only for boarders and a few boys who came each day from distant villages. School dinners on a national scale were unknown then.

Among the after-school activities in which I took part was boxing, for which I was trained by my mother's brother, Sid (he had left the Army and was living at home with Grannie Dockerill). He had been a boxer of some note when he was a Serviceman and I managed to get him taken on by the school as a (voluntary) instructor. I well remember the occasion when the school team gave a display in the Women's Institute Hall and I got carried away with such enthusiasm that my opponent sank to the floor of the ring with blood pouring from his nose – and still I wanted to press home my advantage! "Stop that fight," shouted our head-master, Mr H. Lawrence White, somewhat angrily from his seat in the audience, and, of course, stop it we did. A very short-lived moment of glory for me!

Our other activities at the time included bird-nesting (the illegal practice of collecting the eggs), fruit picking (the Wisbech area is renowned for its strawberries), lots of walks in the area of the Roman Bank (yes, the Romans built it in the days when the Wash extended much further inland), Scouting, cycling and swimming. By today's standards the local swimming pool – or bath, as it was called – was quite primitive. It was on a bank of the tidal River Nene which runs through the town and was emptied and refilled once a week with water taken straight from the river. I cannot remember any such thing as a filtration plant, and I need hardly add that the water was not heated. At school, too, I took part in several Shakespearean plays, usually playing a female role!

After a year or so we moved from Burcroft Road into a new detached house in Oakroyd Crescent. There we had 'all mod cons', even a garage to house the car that my father had by now acquired to use for his business instead of taking trains. This would be about the year 1929 and the first of Dad's several cars was an 11hp *Morris Cowley*. Others included a tourer *Morris Oxford*, a *Clyno* which broke down frequently and a *Jowett*.

By the time I was about 14 I began to take more than a passing interest in motor vehicles. Car engines were far simpler in those days and I soon got the hang of the internal workings of Dad's *Morris*, taking out the sparking plugs to clean and adjust the 'gaps', stripping the carburettor and cleaning out the bowl and jets. Very soon I was behind the steering wheel and backing the car out of the garage, and on trips into the country-side I – quite illegally – gained experience in actual driving, some three years before I was entitled to apply for a licence.

The moment I turned 17 I celebrated by applying for, and getting, that precious document which authorised me to drive. That was in September 1933, the year before a new Traffic Act came into force requiring all *new* applicants to take a driving test. So here I am now at the age of 86 having been a driver for nearly 70 years and never having taken a civilian test! Back in the autumn of 1933 it was a proud moment for me when, in Southport, Lancashire, with my father in the front passenger seat of the *Morris Cowley* and me at the wheel, a policeman approached and demanded to see my licence, probably because I looked very young. I obliged with great speed!

My father with the Morris Cowley at Sandringham in 1932

Me in Southport in 1933

– a proud driving licence holder!

During school holiday periods, when I wasn't at Esher or Exeter, I went with my father on many of his travels to places such as Peterborough, Cambridge, Norwich and Ipswich – even to Felixstowe, little knowing that in later years I would be living there as a family man.

I well remember, too, the night when we were all awakened by a rumbling noise and a rattling of windows and doors. For a few moments the house was actually shaking, then all was very quiet. Yes, it was an earth tremor – I wouldn't describe the occurrence as an earthquake, though it was the nearest approach to one that I have experienced. Fortunately, no damage was done but on going outside we saw a distinct split in the lawn extending for about four yards.

* * * * *

Our next move was to a much smaller house with limited facilities in Osborne Terrace. This must have been at a time when Dad's fortunes were at a low ebb – a dip in the family's financial situation when his job came to an end and he had to seek new employment was invariably the signal for moving house.

Later on, with my father jobless again – the '30s were years of very high unemployment – we moved yet again. This time it was to the *Nene Inn*, a small pub beside the river with living accommodation. The living room was in the basement. My father was the landlord-manager but I think my mother did as much of the work as he did and I well remember the times when I lent a hand in the cellar. Later, when I had left school and become a trainee reporter, my colleagues and I started a local 'Press Club' and enjoyed many a pint in the 'back parlour'.

Though Wisbech was then regarded in other parts of the country as an out-of-the-way place that nobody had ever heard of, it was, in fact, a thriving market town, a busy river port, the capital of the Fens, with plenty of shops and the centre of a flourishing fruit-growing area. There were, believe it or not, two railway stations, one for the LNER (London and North Eastern Railway) line to London via March, the other serving the M&GN line to Peterborough and, again, to London. There are no stations in the town now. Progress?

In the strawberry season train-loads of Cockneys would arrive for the fruit-picking. They were accommodated in huts on the farms and looked after by students from Cambridge. For these Londoners, mainly East Enders, and especially for the children, this annual holiday in the country was a highlight of their year. It must be appreciated that in those days a trip either way was quite an event – for the Londoners, the fresh air and freedom of the countryside; for Wisbechians, perhaps making a long-awaited visit to the capital, the thrill of being in the big city and seeing the sights.

Another annual event was the river swim over an eight-mile course in the tidal River Nene from Sutton Bridge, almost in the Wash, to Wisbech. Crowds lined the Nene quay at the town end to watch the finish of the race, which attracted all the really good swimmers in the area.

Among the notabilities in Wisbech was the Hon. Alexandrina Peckover, who lived in a stately house on the North Brink overlooking the river. Today the house is owned and managed by the National Trust. Another notable figure, going back a lot further in history, was Thomas Clarkson, the slave liberator. One of the 'houses' at the Grammar School bore his name and there is a statue of him in the town centre.

It was while we were living at the *Nene Inn* that I took a special interest in the many ships that sailed the Nene in and out of the port, some bringing in timber from Scandinavia and others loading up with grain. Striking up an acquaintance with a member of one of the crews, I was given a 'Cook's tour' of his ship. The young man was a Norwegian from Tromso. How little did I realise then that some 40 years later my daughter Elizabeth would be marrying a Norwegian and that we would be starting a close association with that beautiful Scandinavian country.

Back to the 1930s, and to the days when, with my father owning a car, we were able to make summer weekend trips to Hunstanton, where Bunty, Una and I enjoyed ourselves, usually with accompanying friends, on the sandy beaches. Our first trip of the season was invariably at Easter when the weather was so cold that Mother stayed in the car and let us youngsters brave the elements!

In Wisbech itself a handsome new stone bridge was built spanning the Nene, replacing an old iron bridge with high sides which I can remember from my earliest days in the town at the beginning of the 1920s. Since then a second bridge has been built about half a mile downstream.

My mother's brother, Sid, was now working in the town's main garage, enabling him to borrow various attractive cars from time to time, and he was always good enough to take me, as a teenager, on trips in the area. This was at the time when two-seater *MG*s came on the scene, though the particular car I recall was a sporty *Rover*. When not actually working in the garage Sid did duty as the driver of the town's 'fever ambulance', the vehicle used to transport infectious cases to the 'fever hospital'.

During part of the school holidays – when not bird-nesting, picking fruit (gooseberries were the worst to handle because the bushes were so prickly) or indulging in other activities with my friends – I spent some time and earned a little money working on the production conveyor belt in a chip-basket factory of which my father knew the owner. It was fun, and profitable, but not the place I wanted to stay in for very long.

One particular incident in my schooldays is still fresh in my mind. I was in the school's Army Cadet Corps and the occasion was a royal visit to the town in the person of the late Prince George, the Duke of Kent, a son of the reigning monarch, King George V. Coming by road, the Prince was delayed by fog for more than an hour and, standing even 'at ease' in the guard which he was to inspect on his arrival was just too much for me. I staggered forward and fell to the ground in a faint. Ignominiously, I had to be carried off in front of the waiting crowd – but I did recover in time to rejoin the ranks for the royal inspection.

During these school years I had a particular friend, Ernest Wright. He was not only clever academically, which I wasn't, but was fortunate to have parents who were in the food business – to be precise, they ran fish-and-chip shops with restaurants attached. This association had the double advantage for me of knowing someone who could, and did, help me with the homework which we did together, and at the same time enable me to enjoy fish and chips free! Many a supper we had, quite late in the evening, during or after we'd done the work which we would have to present at school next day. Once, we decided that, just for the fun of it, we'd stay awake all night and not even make a pretence of going to bed. It seemed a very, very long night, but we made it until dawn broke and hung around for our breakfast before going off to school. I was about 18 or 19 when I lost contact with Ernest in Wisbech, and I didn't see him again until the Grammar School's 600th anniversary celebrations – when I was 63.

We're now in the year 1932. Examinations loomed and along with my friends in the Remove Form (between the Fifth and Sixth Forms) I sat for my School Certificate, more or less the equivalent of today's GCSE. The weeks went by and the day came when I had to scan the columns of *The Daily Telegraph* to see how I had fared. I needn't have bothered. The names of those candidates who had passed and secured the coveted certificate were published, but not those who had failed. My name did not appear, so that was that – I had failed my School Certificate. At that time a candidate had to obtain a credit in at least five subjects; anything less just wouldn't do and there would be no certificate. I had managed to get only four credits – maths, I think, let me down.

Of course, one could take the examination again if one stayed on at school, so my father went to see the headmaster to discuss the situation. The head, Mr White, didn't mince his words. "I think," he said, "that the better course would be for your son to leave at half-term (end of October, 1932) and for you to get him started on a newspaper as that seems to be what he wants to do." Mr White knew of my ambition to become a journalist and may even have seen a copy of a little magazine, *The Fibber*, which I had started as an alternative to the official school publication!

So my fate was sealed. I duly left school in the autumn of 1932, but the *Wisbech Standard*, the local paper which I was to join as an indentured apprentice reporter, could not take me on until the beginning of 1933. In the intervening months I worked in the office of the local income tax collector. My boss kept a large cigarette box on his desk, which was usually quite full, and I must confess that I helped myself to a smoke on more than one occasion! My job at the counter was to accept tax payments (no PAYE then), mainly from local farmers who would get out their chequebooks and write slowly and painstakingly with pens held between their gnarled fingers.

Into Journalism

1933-1939

The months soon passed and the time approached when I was to start on my proper career as a journalist. My choice had been preceded by other options: my grandfather thought I ought to go into the City to train as a stockbroker; the motor industry in Birmingham was another possibility; a third was to join the Merchant Navy as a trainee engine-room artificer. But for some time my own inclination had been towards newspapers, certainly towards news-gathering and presentation, though there was a suggestion that I could become an advertising copywriter.

In the event, after my father had made approaches to other newspapers in the region including the *Eastern Daily Press* in Norwich (the very group now paying my retirement pension!) and the Cambridge paper, it was the *Wisbech Standard* that was to be my training ground. The opposition paper, the *Wisbech Advertiser*, already had one of my slightly older school friends on its reporting staff.

The *Standard* was part of the *Cambridgeshire Times* series, all the papers being printed in March, and it was in the works there that, as an introduction to my training, I started work as a copyholder in the proof-reading department. This entailed travelling to and from March each day by bus – a half-hour journey. Although I actually spent my first few days in the Wisbech office it was the idea of the editor, Mr Ruse, that I would benefit by getting proof-reading experience as a preliminary to my training as a reporter. And he was right, for copy-holding –

that is scanning the original text while another person, the reader, reads aloud the printed text to ensure accuracy – taught me a lot about newspaper style, grammatical construction, paragraphing and so on. After three months I was well versed in the 'art' and ready to try my hand at writing (or typing) reports which actually got into the paper.

Since leaving school I had been attending shorthand and typing classes and I continued these for several more months until I could write shorthand at around 120 words a minute. But I gave up the typing classes, having achieved sufficient skill for the work I had to do, in favour of concentrating on improving my shorthand – regarded as an essential for reporters in those days.

My early reporting days were of a very routine nature. I spent a lot of time 'paragraphing' – that is calling regularly on all kinds of contacts in the town and surrounding villages, mostly people connected with local organisations of some kind, gathering from them information about various activities of a sporting or social nature, then writing up short pieces for inclusion in the paper. Clergymen, clerks to councils, undertakers and club secretaries were among the people I regularly visited, so I got to know them very well and they would ring me up with tit-bits of news.

It may seem strange now, but in the '30s local newspapers in general carried many reports of funerals. The *Wisbech Standard* was no exception and I spent a lot of my time producing quite detailed reports of local deaths – and not only those of prominent people. I think I can safely say that we covered 'the lot', whoever they might have been. I would call on close relatives to obtain details and some people even asked me if I would like to see 'him' or 'her' in the coffin, but I gracefully declined. Then I would attend the funeral, take down the names of everyone present, make notes about the service, look in the grave so that I could describe the coffin and copy out the inscription, take a note of all the wreaths (names and sentiments expressed) and finally, when composing my report, add the name and address of the undertaker. All this, believe it or not, I sometimes did several times a week!

Weddings were another source of news, of course, and again we carried in our columns long reports of all the local ceremonies, detailing relationships and so on, and describing in full the dresses of brides and bridesmaids and the composition of the bouquets.

All these duties I carried out on my own, but for other kinds of reporting engagements I usually accompanied a senior reporter who knew the ropes. One in particular was Frank Owen, the chief reporter and a very competent journalist who took a first-class shorthand note. In later years, after the war, when I joined *The Birmingham Post* as a sub-editor I discovered that Frank was editor of the *Post*'s companion paper, *The Birmingham Evening Mail*; later he became editorial director of *The Post & Mail Company* and he was president of the Guild of British Newspaper Editors at a time when I myself was a member. Small world!

Under the tutelage of Frank Owen and two other senior reporters I learnt how to report court cases, council meetings, shows, fêtes, and all the other events that took place regularly, as well as the unexpected occurrences such as fires, accidents, demonstrations, and so on. A regular job during the summer was coverage of the many 'hospital Sundays' in the villages. These events, lasting most of the day, were held to raise money for the local hospitals (no NHS then) and consisted of assemblies, church or chapel services, fête-like activities and, usually, fireworks. There was plenty for the reporter to do, not the least being to take a shorthand note of the sermon at the church service and the speeches later on. These events played havoc with what would otherwise have been free time and there was no overtime to recompense me. My salary then as an apprentice reporter was only five shillings (25p) a week, and one didn't get very fat on that, even allowing for the different values of those times.

Time for yet another house move – from the *Nene Inn* to Park Road (not so grand as it sounds). Bunty had by now left school and started a clerical job with a printing company; Una was still at the Convent School. It was during this period that we came to know the Rodgers family in which Anton (of TV and stage fame) was then just a baby. Today his face is familiar to millions. Mr Rodgers worked, I think I am right in saying, for a firm of accountants, Mrs Rodgers ran a small concert party, and Anton had five sisters. The family lived in Opportune Road, Wisbech, so called because the builder of most of the houses in the immediate area had his own home facing that road – and his name was Tune! Anton, who is particularly remembered for his leading roles in *May to December* (1989), *Fresh Fields* (1984), *French Fields* and *Noah's Ark,* has been a guest star in many other productions, including *Rumpole of the Bailey, Upstairs Downstairs, Midsomer Murders,* and *Return of the Saint.*

Bunty became a member of Mrs Rodgers' concert party, which gave performances in village halls and at the *Electric Cinema* in the town. I helped with stage lighting, a job which suited me particularly well when the shows were in the cinema as I was friendly with Edna, the daughter of the owners, a Mr and Mrs Gough, and she worked as the upstairs usherette. Small-scale rehearsals were often held in the front room of the Rodgers' house, with Mrs Rodgers thumping away at the piano, a *Park Drive* cigarette dangling from her mouth, the ash about to fall on to the keys, and the packet close at hand at the end of the keyboard! Anton was far too young to remember such scenes but my description is a true one.

In another musical sphere in the mid-'30s my mother was in the chorus of the Wisbech Operatic Society which performed several Gilbert and Sullivan operas on the stage of the town's *Empire Theatre*. She also took part in a spectacular pageant which depicted Wisbech through the ages.

Meanwhile my reporting activities continued – courts, inquests, council meetings, accidents, fires, fêtes and the inevitable funerals. Whenever there was a fire the volunteer local fire brigade was alerted by the firing of a 'maroon' on the river bank outside the police station. The very loud bang could be heard for miles. One Saturday night there was a particularly extensive farm fire and having turned out on hearing the maroon I drove to the scene of the blaze and got all the details I needed. I then telephoned a report to one of the national Sunday papers – probably the *Sunday Express*. This was my first effort in the 'linage' field, the term being used to describe contributions from freelance reporters and the amount of the payment made depending largely on the number of lines the report made in the paper.

The General Election of 1935 gave me my first experience of political reporting, though in earlier elections my father had helped with canvassing and I had gained some knowledge of party politics. Wisbech was in the Isle of Ely constituency and the sitting MP was Mr James A. de Rothschild (of the famous wealthy family). On his re-election, ropes would be attached to his beautiful Rolls-Royce and, sitting in the car with his wife beside him, he would be towed in triumph through the town. His wife, I remember, had a lovely car of her own (not so common then) – a very sporty *AC*.

The *Wisbech Standard* was also interested in electioneering in part of adjacent Norfolk, and it was after covering an evening meeting in a village between Wisbech and Kings Lynn that I was involved in my first road accident. With me at the time was my old school friend, Tom Walton, a big chap with long legs. Driving back after the meeting, in the dark and along a typically bleak Fenland road, I was suddenly confronted by a large lorry whose driver was attempting to turn his vehicle which completely blocked the road. With dykes either side there was no escape route, and all I could do was to slam on the brakes and hope for the best. But the brakes of the firm's *Singer* van, like the lights, left much to be desired and before we knew it we had crashed into the side of the lorry. I was lucky to escape without a scratch but Tom's knees were jammed against the dashboard, fortunately without any serious effect.

Somehow we got back to Wisbech after abandoning the van, and the next morning it was with some trepidation that I reported to the editor on our night's adventure. Mr Ruse was anything but pleased, to put it mildly, and took some convincing that the accident was not my fault. In the end, however, he accepted that the lorry should not have been blocking the road without a warning light being shown, and when the police came to the office to take a statement he backed me up and there was no prosecution – at any rate no charge was made against me. Of course the van was a write-off – and we were all delighted to get a nice new *Morris* as a replacement!

There came a time when we were persuaded to join the National Union of Journalists. This didn't suit our employers at all because it meant, in the main, increasing reporters' pay to the level agreed nationally by the Newspaper Society, the employers' organisation, and the union. Lengthy negotiations took place and I remember Clem Bundock, the union's colourful general secretary, coming down from London for meetings with us journalists and the company's representatives. An agreement was eventually hammered out but the worst was soon to come, for the chief reporter, George Martin, was sacked.

This move by the company was regarded by the union as victimisation and no time was lost in calling us all out on strike. All except me, that is, for the union accepted that as an indentured apprentice I was legally bound to do what I was told by my employers and could not refuse to work. That was all very well but it meant that a heavy workload descended on the editor (also exempt from striking) and myself: in fact, I suppose it was good for me since I found myself sharing the coverage, in great detail, of such assignments as the meeting of the Town Council and similar important events.

In due course the dispute was settled and everyone resumed working. From then on the NUJ was recognised by the company and agreed rates were paid. Incidentally, the senior minimum was then £4-7s 6d (£4.37½) a week! I think the Fleet Street rate was nine guineas (£9.45). Times have changed!

* * * * *

Towards the end of 1935 I felt sufficiently competent to think about applying for a reporting post elsewhere. My indentures were for five years of which I had so far completed barely three. Nevertheless my employers agreed to release me if I managed to secure another job. This I did, answering an advertisement in *The Daily Telegraph* and corresponding with the editor of the *Surrey Weekly Press* in Guildford, who was seeking a second reporter (there was only one other). I was not asked to attend for an interview and on the strength of my letter of application, backed up by a reference from the *Standard* editor, Mr Ruse, I was appointed to the job.

This must have caused some discussion and quick thinking within the family because in no time my father decided to give up whatever he was then doing – if anything very remunerative at all – and leave Wisbech with me to seek another job in or near London. Mother and the girls were, for the time being, to

60

remain in Wisbech. So Dad and I duly set off by train for Surbiton, where my grandparents were then living just off the road to Tolworth, a convenient place from which my father could travel by train to London each day and I could go in the opposite direction to Guildford.

It escapes me just how long Dad stayed with his parents, what job he secured in London or how long it lasted. For me the daily journey to and from Guildford ended after a fortnight; by then I had found lodgings with the mother of a young man who worked in the advertising department of the newspaper. His name was Cecil Bartlet, or Barty as we called him. In later years, after the war, he founded his own very successful advertising agency.

It was on a Monday early in January 1936 that I reported for duty at the office of the *Surrey Weekly Press* in Chapel Street, Guildford, the very day on which the nation learned with great sorrow of the death of King George V. I couldn't have been thrown into a deeper 'deep end' for I was quickly involved in various reporting assignments associated with a royal death, reactions to the news and the proclamation of the new King, Edward VIII (later to become the Duke of Windsor), from the steps of Guildford's then pro-Cathedral, the Church of the Holy Trinity, in the town's High Street.

I soon settled down to reporting in Guildford, and beyond to Godalming, my 'district' which I covered on a bicycle and where I made all the various calls for news items in the same way as I had done in the Wisbech area. In Guildford itself I was in daily contact with the police and fire brigade and reported cases in Guildford Magistrates' Court, held in the ancient Guildhall halfway up the cobbled High Street. The paper's chief reporter (remember I was the number two) was Frank Attridge, and he and I began a friendship which continued into the war years and beyond.

Very soon my father, working in London, managed to obtain the tenancy of a brand new semi-detached house in Joseph's Road, Guildford, opposite the city football ground. We named it *Fenholme* after the Cambridgeshire Fenlands. Mother and the girls left Wisbech and we were soon together again. Bunty got a job in the office of *Dennis Bros*, the lorry, bus and fire engine manufacturers, whose factory was on the outskirts of the town, and it was there that she met Arthur Harris, who was to become my brother-in-law four years later. Arthur was then living with his widowed mother and sister, Rene, in Old Palace Road, only a few hundred yards from 26 Elmside, Onslow Village, which has been his and Bunty's home for nearly sixty years.

Bunty and Arthur, Frank Attridge and I had quite a large circle of young friends, and at weekends we did a lot of walking – on the Hog's Back, at Newlands Corner and along the leafy lanes of Surrey. Often we would end up at *Somerset Farm* where, for what would be a pittance today, we enjoyed strawberry teas. We also went to Imps' dances at nearby Merrow (the Imps were members of the Conservative Party's Junior Imperial League) and to other 'hops' in Guildford, usually in the Public Hall in North Street, now part of a shopping complex. I well remember evening snacks – invariably eggs and chips – which we had in a little café up several flights of stairs above a corner shop opposite the hall. We drank, too, in various local pubs, mostly in *Henekeys* in the High Street, where we could get a half-pint of draught *Bass* for 5d (less than 2½p).

Aside from the proclamation of the new King, the biggest event of my years in Guildford was the laying of the foundation stone of Guildford Cathedral in 1937 by the then Archbishop of Canterbury, Cosmo Lang. This was a very great occasion in a national, as well as local, sense for the new Cathedral was the first to be built in England since the days of the Reformation, and there was a huge number of dignitaries and people from all walks of life assembled around the earlier-erected wooden cross on Stag Hill for the historic ceremony.

I particularly remember the official luncheon which followed because I didn't go to it! Unlike the reporters from some of the media, the *Surrey Weekly Press* did not receive an invitation, but we were expected to obtain copies of the speeches and print them (which we did, of course, though under protest). The Cathedral itself was less than half built two years later when the war broke out, and it was not until some years after the war that this magnificent building was completed.

Another notable occasion was in 1938 when a National Fire Brigades event in the town coincided with Guildford Carnival. Bunty had been persuaded to enter a competition to select the Carnival Queen and had won. So it was Queen Bunty who, flanked by the Carnival Princesses, rode atop a fire engine through the streets of the town to the acclamation of the crowds.

The *Surrey Weekly Press* was the smallest of three papers in Guildford, the others being the *Surrey Advertiser* and the *Surrey Times*. Eventually, after I had left the paper, the *Surrey Weekly Press* was absorbed by the *Surrey Times*, and years later the *Times* itself was absorbed by the larger *Advertiser*. In my time the *Advertiser*'s premises were in the centre of the town, in Market Street. Later a modern building, very much in the 1930s' style, was erected a short distance away in Martyr Road. This housed the paper's offices and printing works until very recent times when everything was moved out of the central area to new premises on the fringe of the town on the Woking Road.

Frank and I were, of course, friendly with the reporters on the other papers. One, whose name was Reynolds – we called him Rennie – was a very competent journalist who took a good short-hand note. He was also a heavy drinker (not unusual among newspapermen of the day), and it was said of him that if he'd had a few before taking notes he would have to imbibe freely again when he later had to transcribe them, otherwise he couldn't decipher his shorthand! Another reporter was an even more expert shorthand writer, so much so that he eventually left the town to join the shorthand-writing team in the House of Commons, where 100 per cent accuracy at the highest speeds was essential.

During those pre-war days in Guildford, in the summer, we all frequented the Lido, a large open-air swimming pool set in the attractive surroundings of the town's Stoke Park. The water was, I'm sure, unheated but that did not deter us young people from going there for a swim at the earliest opportunity in the season.

Frank and I occasionally went to London. One trip was to the then *Sunday Chronicle*, where one of our former Guildford colleagues was on the reporting staff. To say we had quite a night would be to put it mildly; in fact, we downed so much beer, and I had omitted to visit the loo before we caught the train at Waterloo, that I had to disembark, with Frank, when we got as far as Weybridge. Of course, by the time I was in a fit state to resume the journey the train had long since departed, so we began the walk to Guildford. Very fortunately for us, after a mile or so a kind lady motorist stopped and gave us a lift. I don't think that would happen today.

On another visit to London we plucked up courage and went into a night club, passing burly bouncers at the door. Inside, two girls soon attached themselves to us and expected expensive drinks. Somehow we managed to avoid buying them anything and just ordered two beers, which would have cost us about 9d (3¾p) in Guildford. Imagine our horror when we had to fork out 8s 6d (42½p) – about 13 times as much! We then beat a hasty retreat – probably the club staff were as glad to get rid of us as we were to escape!

On another occasion, nearer home, we went to a New Year's Eve Dance in Godalming and did the conga in the High Street.

I think Bunty and Arthur were with us then. We really did have a lot of fun in those days.

In September 1937 I celebrated my 21st birthday by taking my younger sister Una, then aged 11, to the pictures. Strange to say, perhaps, I had no actual girl-friend at the time, though Frank and I did know and go around with several females. A bonus on my birthday was the £100 – a fortune to me then – that I inherited from my late mother. I immediately used about £20 of this to buy a second-hand 1929 *Austin Seven* car for £15 and to tax and insure it with the remaining £5. The car came from a garage in Hampshire run by a distant relative of Grannie Dockerill, so I took it to be a good buy and in perfect running order.

Within a day or so I was brave enough to set out for Exeter, some 170 miles away, in this little car which would do about 35 mph. All went well until I was about 50 miles from Exeter, then a tyre burst. I managed to fit the spare and continued the journey to my Uncle Willie's. Next day we scoured the junk yards looking for a used replacement tyre and managed to find one that was just the right size. I bought it for the incredible sum of two shillings and sixpence (12½p).

It was with great pride that I took my uncle and Aunt Marion (Aunty Edie had died), for a ride into the Devonshire countryside, having had first to remove the sparking plugs for cleaning, then to warm them on the gas stove so that the engine would start. Even so, the little *Austin* couldn't make it up some of the hills with the three of us in it, so Auntie and Uncle had to get out to lighten the load and push! Though I don't remember much about the return journey to Guildford I do know that the car made it safely.

Another problem I had with the *Austin* was with the universal joint connecting the engine to the prop shaft. This flexible joint was made of some kind of fibre and on my car it had a habit of tearing. Fortunately, I kept the car garaged at a house only a few doors away from home, and even more fortunately this garage had an inspection pit, so I was able to get under the car to remove the universal joint and fit a new one each time there was any trouble.

After a while I decided to sell the car. Frank Attridge had bought a motor-cycle, a 250cc machine which he had ordered by post and which came by rail to Guildford Station in a wooden crate – all, I'm fairly sure, for the sum of £29-10s. It was Frank who urged me to get rid of the car and buy a motor-cycle, like him. So the *Austin* went to a distant cousin of my father's who lived at Claygate, near Surbiton, and I got exactly £15 back for it!

I saw the bike I fancied, a 250cc *Aerial Red Hunter*, which, although secondhand, was a superior machine to Frank's. I bought it for £40 and took my mother along to the showroom when I went to pay for it and collect it. She was quite horrified when she saw the machine and had visions of me tearing about the countryside on it.

Meanwhile my reporting activities continued apace. One day a councillor approached me to ask if I would take a verbatim note of a forthcoming Town Council meeting and let him have a typed report. As I recall it, he was in dispute with some other members of the council over a matter which the authority had been discussing. At any rate, anxious to earn an extra bob or two, I readily agreed and duly put my shorthand to the test by taking a full note of the relevant council proceedings. Then I spent most of the night in the office transcribing my notes. I cannot remember how much the councillor paid me but I am sure the effort was worth it.

By now Frank Attridge had decided to make a move and he left Guildford to join the reporting staff of the *Hastings Observer*. We kept in close touch and I remember a holiday I spent with

Frank in Hastings during which we went on a day trip to France – my first taste of a foreign country.

At this time the *Surrey Weekly Press* was making little, if any, profit, so I don't suppose it came as much of a surprise to us when the sole proprietor decided to sell it. He found a buyer in a company which had its own printing works and published a series of weekly papers in the Walthamstow area of East London. The first thing the new owners did was to get rid of the editor, a charming elderly man named Gordon – he departed to Wales, to a sub-editing job on the evening paper in Swansea – and replace him with a much younger journalist from their own stable. Under him the presentation of the paper undoubtedly improved. He had some good ideas and the paper was printed on a modern rotary press as opposed to the 'flat-bed' machine use by the contract printers in Guildford.

During the week copy was sent to the printing works at Walthamstow either by train or post, or it was taken by hand. Every Thursday I travelled to East London by train, via Waterloo and Liverpool Street, to spend the day in the printing works while the Linotype setting of the last batches of copy was completed and the assembling of the pages was carried out. My job was to cut reports to fit and check all the pages before the press rolled and the papers spewed out.

By this time it would be very late at night and the advertising manager would have arrived from Guildford by car, into which the two of us, with the help of the pressroom staff, loaded the entire print run. Then, in the early hours, it was off back to Surrey by road, dropping off parcels of papers at points in and around Guildford before I was deposited in Joseph's Road to crawl into bed.

* * * * *

So the weeks went by, until one day the company, a non-union concern (then, at any rate), having become aware that I belonged to the NUJ, told me that if I were to remain in its employment I would have to leave the union. I was even offered an alternative job at the Walthamstow office, still with the proviso that I left the NUJ. There was no chance at all of my doing this and I was given the full backing of the union. So the answer to my employers was, "No, thank you," and my time with the *Surrey Weekly Press* came to an end.

That was in 1938 and for about six weeks I was out of work, but not out of pocket, for I received not only State unemployment pay but benefit from the union. I was even a bit better off financially!

Jobs for young journalists were then few and far between. One that I applied for unsuccessfully was with the *Reading Evening Gazette*. In the end I was taken on by the *Surrey County Herald* at Sutton. Again, as at Guildford, this was the smallest of three papers covering the area, the others being the *Croydon Advertiser* and the *Croydon Times*. Apart from reporting in Sutton itself I covered a district which included Ewell, near Epsom, North and South Cheam and Worcester Park, all typical London suburbs.

As a family we were still living in Guildford, so each day I had to travel to Sutton and back on my motor-bike. The 'leathers' of today's motor-cycling fraternity were unknown then, and I wore voluminous 'waders' (similar to the garb which anglers wear standing in water), a waterproof leather-style coat, a leather helmet (à la aviators), goggles and gauntlet gloves. I was even able to put all that lot on over an evening suit and to step out at the end of a long ride quite immaculately dressed! The motor-bike was, of course, a great improvement on the old office bicycle as a means of transport to reporting assignments as well as getting me to work and back.

Inevitably another house move was in the offing – a case of 'everywhere that Tony went the family was sure to go', and that only came to an end when the war broke out! So before long we all departed from Guildford and settled in a Victorian house in Cecil Road, Cheam, not far from the centre of Sutton. I think my father continued working in London, but Bunty had to leave *Dennis Bros.* and find another job, ending up also working in London.

Life in and around Sutton was not so very different from what it had been in Guildford, though there were more recreational amenities but not the immediate attractive countryside. Streatham ice rink was not far away and there was a roller skating rink in Sutton, both of which I went to many times. Eventually Frank Attridge decided to leave Hastings and join me as a reporter, for the Wallington area, on the *County Herald* and he joined me on these outings. As we had a roomy house and my own bedroom was more than large enough for me, Frank moved in with us as a paying guest, an arrangement which suited everyone very well.

We were close enough to London to be able to go to events there quite easily. I took my mother to the Radio Show – either at Earls Court or Olympia, I forget which – and there, for the first time, we saw rows of television sets in operation. Television transmission had started in Britain in 1935 when the transmitter was at Crystal Palace, but very few people had sets before the war. One who did was the Roman Catholic priest at North Cheam whom I visited regularly for news items. His set, like most others of the time, was very large but the screen was quite tiny. I think it was of the reflective type, that is, the cathode ray tube pointed up towards a vertical screen from which the picture was reflected to the viewer. Large squares of magnifying glass were also used with sets of that era.

A memorable family event of the time was the celebration of my grandparents' Golden Wedding when we all went to London in a hired limousine.

My grandparents' Golden Wedding in 1939
Standing: Tony, Bunty, Una, my father
Seated: Grandpa, Grandma, my stepmother

After dinner at a posh restaurant – the famous singer Hutch (Leslie Hutchinson) was at the piano – we were driven round the brightly-lit central area of the capital before returning home. I had earlier taken advantage of my grandfather's long association with the City of London, and his marked sense of punctuality, by sending a story to one of the national papers relating how, for at least 40 years when living at Esher, he had walked across the Common to the station at such an exact time each day that the local residents kept a look out for him so as to set their clocks and watches! I don't think it pleased my grandfather when the tabloid to which I had sent the story displayed placards at the station proclaiming in very large letters, 'Surbiton's Human Clock', and used much the same wording for the headline to the report in the paper. They got it wrong, of course, because if anything grandfather had been 'Esher's Human Clock'.

Early Days of World War II

1939-1941

We were now in the fateful year of 1939 and on the political scene things were hotting up. Hitler and his Nazis had already dealt with the Sudetenland and Austria and in 1938 had invaded Czechoslovakia. There was little doubt that sooner or later – probably sooner – we were going to be involved in another war with Germany. Rearming had been proceeding apace after the years of *dis*armament, but we still had a lot of catching up to do. The organisation of a system of air raid precautions, involving shelters and the like, was under way and people were advised to buy materials to make blackout curtains.

In principle we should have gone to the aid of the Czechs, but in 1938 we were ill-prepared for war. The intervening year gave us the opportunity to go some way towards catching up with Germany and the mood in the country encouraged recruiting to the Armed Services, especially the Territorial Army and the Naval and Air Reserves. Young men and women like Bunty and me – she was coming up to 21 and I was nearing 23 – flocked to the back-up services in the early months of 1939.

I think it was my friend and former colleague, Barty, from Guildford days, who was the first of my acquaintances to join a Royal Tank Regiment Territorial battalion, and it was his lead that prompted me, and then Frank Attridge, to follow suit. With the completion of recruitment to the 42nd, 48 RTR had just been formed, and it was, therefore, the 48th that Frank and I joined at Clapham Common. We would drive over from Cheam on one or two evenings a week for drill and training. I say 'drive' because by now I had disposed of my *Aerial* motorbike and bought a second-hand three-wheeler car. It was a *BSA* which had two-wheel drive at the front and a single wheel at the rear, unlike the famous *Morgan* which had chain drive to the rear wheel, and the three-wheelers of post-war years which had (and still have) one wheel at the front and two at the back. About the same time Bunty joined the ATS (Auxiliary Territorial Service) at Sutton.

With my three-wheeler BSA in 1938

My father was delighted to see us both in uniform. A very patriotic man, he was still on the Reserve of Officers from the 1914-18 conflict, and when the war did eventually break out he was summoned to somewhere in Whitehall. He came home a very disappointed man, for because of his deafness he was turned down for service. I have always felt that this was not merely unjust to him but it deprived the Army of a former officer of only 48 with a lot of military experience, who could have been most useful in a desk job at least.

His deafness had started when he was in his early thirties and operations had proved ineffective. So for the rest of his life he had to wear a hearing-aid, without which he could hear practically nothing. Compared with the sophisticated instruments of today the aids of those days were very basic and cumbersome, with large headphones and equally obtrusive microphones. It was, of course, my father's deafness which had counted against him when it came to getting a job, as with high unemployment in the inter-war years his chances were greatly reduced when other applicants were not so afflicted. Ironically his most successful working years were between 1939 and 1945 when the vast majority of young men were either in the Services or on war work, though normal trading was, of course, at a low ebb.

On the international stage a glimmer of hope had appeared towards the end of 1938 when the Prime Minister, Neville Chamberlain, had returned from Munich after a meeting with Hitler and, as he stepped from his plane, flourished a piece of paper and declared that he believed there would be 'peace for our time'. But we were used to Hitler's broken promises and put little faith in it. As the months passed Britain and France pledged to go to the aid of Poland in the event of an attack, so the inevitability of war came as no surprise when the Nazis invaded Poland at 5.45 am on 1st September 1939.

During August of that year 48 RTR had been in camp near Aldershot, the Army's largest base, for 14 days. There, as a trooper despatch rider with a *BSA* machine, I got my first taste of Army life. We learnt how to operate *Vickers* machine-guns and to drive tanks and tracked personnel carriers. On returning to work in Sutton my first job was to write an account of my experiences for the paper – I think it ran to about two columns.

Within days, on that Friday of September, urgent announcements were transmitted on the radio by the *BBC*, calling on all Servicemen and women, Regulars, Reservists and Territorials, to report to their depots as soon as possible. That evening Bunty and I did our packing in readiness for responding to the call early the next morning, and I phoned my editor to tell him that I had been called up. To my amazement, he informed me that I couldn't possibly respond as he had me down in the diary to cover a meeting on the following Monday! That didn't cut any ice with me, of course, and I told him in no uncertain terms that I had no choice but to join my regiment. That, then, was the end of my reporting career for the next six-and-a-half years.

* * * * *

The next morning, Saturday 2nd September, Bunty and I departed for our respective depots at Dover Castle and Clapham Common. This was to mark the end of our family life at home, though neither of us appreciated that at the time, of course.

Arriving at Clapham – it must have been by bus or train because I had to leave my car behind – I found myself in the midst of great activity, with several hundred others reporting for duty and many 'impressed' (commandeered or hired) vehicles milling around. I would describe the scene as one of organised chaos! By the evening we had been sorted into groups to spend the night lying on the floors of empty rooms in the large old house which the regiment occupied. Blankets were issued and food was brought in from various cafés and restaurants in the area.

We made an early start next morning, Sunday 3rd September, piling into civilian trucks and heading for Sanderstead, a very pleasant outer suburb of Croydon, which was not too far distant. On arrival our officers were soon very busy calling at houses to secure billets for us all. The residents had little choice – there was no question of anyone being allowed to refuse to take us in, though I imagine the officers were understanding and used their common sense if they called at a home which was already overcrowded, and no doubt the inhabitants of Sanderstead had been pre-warned of the imminent arrival of troops.

I was one of a group of three to be billeted with a newly-married couple in a nice house which they had only just started to furnish. But that didn't matter, for all they had to provide for us was shelter and toilet and washing facilities. There were three or four bedrooms and we had our own blankets. Meals would be provided by our own cooks, and a cookhouse and eating area were quickly established in a local hall.

While all these preparations were being made we literally lounged about on the streets, and it was while I was sitting on a kerb listening to the radio – this time really marked the start of almost continuous news broadcasting – that I heard the fateful announcement by the Prime Minister. In familiar measured tones Neville Chamberlain told the world that, Hitler and the Nazi government having failed to respond to an ultimatum which had expired at 11.00 am, "...this country is now at war with Germany." That was it then, the war was on – and who could say when it would end?

Trained British troops – Regulars, Reservists and Territorials – were soon on the Continent, joining forces with the French, while the Royal Navy and the RAF swung into action too, leaving the rest of us to start serious training for the time when we would be ready to play our part. At that time the 48th had to make do with somewhat outdated equipment, but as time went on and armament factories stepped up production we got modern weaponry and vehicles. The early months were aptly called the 'phoney war' because not a great deal happened and there was little aerial activity, though from Day One the air raid sirens would occasionally sound – usually for false alarms.

But the war took a different turn in the spring of 1940. In April the Nazis invaded Denmark and Norway and in May Holland and Belgium surrendered – only a week or so after an over-confident Chamberlain told the British Parliament that Hitler had 'missed the bus'. Very fortunately for us all he soon handed over to Winston Churchill, and in June Allied forces were evacuated from Dunkirk after being encircled by the Germans, who had skirted round one end of the much-vaunted Maginot Line. German troops paraded in Paris and on 22nd June the French signed an armistice.

For the next year and a half Britain virtually stood alone, until the United States entered the war after the bombing of its fleet at Pearl Harbour on 7th December 1941. It would be truer to say, of course, that the countries of the British Empire and Colonies, together with Norwegians, Dutch, Belgians, French, Poles and others who had managed to escape from occupied Europe, all joined us in the fight – and many of them gave their lives.

The 48th remained at Sanderstead until the spring of 1940. Training proceeded apace and we actually got some tanks. Apart from an occasional spell working in the cookhouse – not, I should add, as a cook but as a washer-and-cleaner-up – I was given a truck to drive and made regular journeys into central London for supplies of various kinds. We drivers painted the letters WD (War Department) on our 'impressed' civilian vehicles, put our feet down and paid little heed to some of the rules of the road. A bit heady!

Technical courses were soon underway and an early one for me was in driving and maintenance (D and M) when we learnt a lot about the mechanics of both wheeled and tracked vehicles, petrol and diesel engines and, for instance, epicyclic gears. For diesels we worked at a London Transport garage on the engines and transmissions of buses.

One day a few of us were moving a complete engine by hand and I was slow to take my hand away when it was being lowered on to a bench. The result was that the tip of the third finger of my right hand was very smartly cut off. Little did I realise at that moment that this mishap, and its consequences, were to shape the rest of my life – as will be seen in due course.

I was taken to Croydon Hospital, where, under anaesthetic, I had the wound dressed and sewn, leaving the hospital with instructions to report daily to the regiment's MI (medical inspection) room for the wounded finger to be re-dressed. This I duly did, to have the dressing seen to each time by the medical officer's orderly, or 'nurse', a Lance-corporal John Mumford. Perhaps the rest can be imagined. John, whom I had not known personally before, became my best friend (after Frank Attridge) and he it was who, in the autumn of 1940, introduced me to the Meadlarklan family.

*　*　*　*　*

In the early months of 1940 it was generally feared that the Germans would launch an invasion. Had they done so I would undoubtedly have had a very different story to tell – if I were allowed to tell it. It could be said that from their point of view that was the time when *they* 'missed the bus'.

In Britain every precaution was taken to deal with possible landings, though still with very limited resources. The 48th left Sanderstead for coastal outposts in Essex and for a time were in barracks in Colchester as the time approached when Hitler, through Goering and the Luftwaffe, would launch his blitzkrieg against England – and we all know what the blitz did. But aside from the immense damage and great loss of life the effect was to stiffen the resistance and resolve of the British people.

Within weeks, as the blitz gathered momentum, we left Essex for the comparative safety of Salisbury Plain. Now we were under canvas and the regiment was equipped with its first brand new tanks, diesel-powered *Valentines*. They were relatively fast tanks but, like most other British armoured vehicles of that time, their guns were under-powered.

I became a tank driver for the Commanding Officer and for the next few months of the summer while German bombs were raining down on the cities and towns of England, with industrial centres such as Coventry as well as London under constant attack, and the Battle of Britain was being fought in the air, the regiment engaged in battle manoeuvres on the plain.

Bunty at Cheam in 1939

John Mumford at Sanderstead

My friendship with John Mumford continued and whenever possible we went out together to sink welcome pints at pubs in the nearby villages, often having to walk several miles to find them.

As the autumn of 1940 approached the Battle of Britain reached its climax, with ever larger numbers of German aircraft being shot down, albeit at the cost of many *Spitfires* and *Hurricanes* and their young pilots. It was then, when we were winning the war in the air and the Germans had to accept the fact that they would never defeat us by aerial attack, that 48 RTR made its next move. This time it was to Suffolk, where the regiment was to be based for the next year or more in the extensive grounds of *Glevering Hall* on the outskirts of Wickham Market. In the wooded area surrounding the parkland concrete hard standings had been laid for our tanks: these, it may be surprising to learn, are there to this day, though most are now partly hidden by vegetation.

Throughout the severe winter our living accommodation was in bell tents as we helped with the work of building wooden huts. Officers were housed in the mansion, where our administrative offices were also set up. A large cowshed became our mess hall and after our meals we washed up individually in an open tank of cold water to which antiseptic crystals had been added. So hygienic! Heating, such as it was, was provided by a smelly coke stove in the centre of the building, its chief virtue being that we could stand round it to make toast on which we spread thick layers of margarine and jam.

* * * * *

Shortly after our arrival in Suffolk John Mumford told me that before the war he had visited friends who lived in Felixstowe. This was news to me but it appeared he had known Marjorie Meadlarklan in London, where they both worked. Leonard Cuming, who married Marjorie in 1939, was a Regular in the RAF and at that time serving in the Far East. Hence John's association with the Meadlarklan family.

That day, leaving me to my own devices in Wickham Market, John made his way to Felixstowe to see them, but when he called at the house in Princes Road where he had stayed with the 'Meads' (as everyone called them) he found the Army in occupation! On making enquiries of the neighbours he learnt that the family had moved inland to Needham Market, so it was to Needham that he hurried by bus via Ipswich.

As he expected, the Meads gave him a wonderfully friendly welcome, which was typical of them for not only were they very pleased to see him personally but theirs was 'open house' to Servicemen in the area. This visit was on a Sunday and John needed no persuasion whatsoever in accepting an invitation to pay another visit the following weekend. He asked if he could bring a friend, quite certain that he would receive the favourable reply that, in fact, he did.

The next Sunday John and I made our way by Army transport into Ipswich and thence by bus to Needham and to the Meads' centuries-old house in the High Street (later destroyed in a bombing raid). At the time, late September or early October 1940, there were at home George Meadlarklan and his wife, Gertrude, and their children: Marjorie (by then married to Leonard, in the RAF, and expecting her first child), Kathleen (engaged to Cyril Rogers, in the Fire Service), Audrey, Greta (recovering from an appendix operation), Bernard (then 14 or 15) and Anne, aged 6. The eldest daughter, Brenda, was married to Alan Howard and lived in Norfolk, and brother Jack, in the Royal Army Service Corps, was 21.

I was given as warm a welcome as John had received and found Mr and Mrs Meadlarklan very lovable people to whom I quickly formed an attachment. From the start I was made to feel one of the family..., which was just as well because on my first glimpse of daughter No.4 – yes, Audrey – I could hardly take my eyes off her. If ever there was a case of love at first sight this was it, as far as I was concerned, though it probably took a little longer for Audrey to reciprocate my feelings. Actually, I think it was John who had hopes of becoming closer to her now that Marjorie was married, and he thought that I might be drawn towards her friend from Felixstowe, Olive Pinner (then in the WAAF), when I met her later. But it was not to be!

This was one of many regular visits to Needham, and Audrey and I soon formed a close relationship. But I did have a serious rival, a Sergeant Bowman serving in a Scottish regiment in the town, who had known Audrey for a while.

Audrey aged 10 in her ballet dress

Grade 1 Certificate

George and Gertrude Meadlarklan in 1949

Pre-war home of the 'Meads' in Felixstowe
It is still a private residence

It was at Christmas, 1940, when John and I were right royally entertained by the Meads, that I noticed my regimental Christmas card to the family was creased and bore very dirty marks. The explanation was that the said Sergeant Bowman, on seeing my card, had removed it from the mantelshelf, put it on the floor and stamped on it with his Army boots. This did him no good at all, whatever satisfaction it may have given him, and I venture to say that it not only diminished his chances but considerably improved mine. From that time onwards Sergeant Bowman began to fade from the picture and my relationship with Audrey became closer.

The Meadlarklans had moved to Needham Market some months earlier in 1940. Like other families in Felixstowe, they had left the town on Government and local advice because of the possibility of a German invasion. Posters were put up warning of this danger and suggesting that those people who had no special reason for remaining in the town – for example, being employed locally – and especially families with young children, should move further inland.

Some time before the Meads left Felixstowe, Audrey and her sister Kaye were out on the Prom one evening and managed to get seaward of the barbed wire barrier that had been set up to delay (it couldn't have been more than that) any follow-up to an enemy landing. They were soon apprehended by armed patrolling troops (full marks for security!) and taken to Landguard Fort, then occupied by the Army, and held for a time in the guardroom. I'm sure they found it quite exciting! At any rate, a phone call to the Meads' home enabled their identity to be confirmed and they were released and taken home, I believe in Army transport.

* * * * *

In the summer of 1940 I had been unable to get leave to attend Bunty and Arthur's wedding in Guildford. Bunty had been able to leave the ATS because her husband-to-be was on war work, and when they married she and Arthur moved into Arthur's mother's bungalow, 12 Elmside, Onslow Village, barely 100 yards from their present home, No.26 Elmside. By this time my mother and father, with Una, had left Cheam and returned to Guildford, firstly into rooms off Farnham Road, then to other rooms off Woodbridge Road. Later on they obtained the tenancy of a house of their own in Manor Gardens, which became the family home for the rest of my father's life and, for a number of years, that of Grannie Dockerill, too. Una was married from Manor Gardens.

Back in Suffolk John Mumford and I spent the Christmas of 1940 as guests of the Meads at 47 High Street, Needham Market. One of the highlights of our stay was the exciting (to us) game of 'Sardines'. All the young people joined in: one of us had to leave the room and hide, and after an agreed interval everyone else dispersed to look for this person; on finding him, or her, one remained in the hiding place until, eventually, everyone was squashed together in a small space. I suppose it would be regarded as 'old hat' today but for us the game was sheer delight, and we continued to play it in later years when the Meads moved up the street to *Rose Villa*.

Audrey and I saw each other as much as possible, i.e. as frequently as military duties permitted. We used to meet in Ipswich, have a cup of tea at *Lyons* and go to the pictures. I well remember the first film we saw together: it was *The Magic Bullet,* starring Edward G. Robinson, at the *Ritz* in the Buttermarket. The cinema has gone now and been replaced by a branch of *British Home Stores*.

On one evening we were caught in an air raid. The Germans were dropping bombs on Ipswich docks and we could hear them whistling down as we huddled together in a doorway on the Cornhill. I must have felt very anxious when I put Audrey on her bus for Needham Market before boarding Army transport to return to *Glevering Hall.*

Most of the buses were gas-powered via coke-burning apparatus carried in trailers, and it was all they could do to get up the hill at Whitton when going into Ipswich. A lot of the buses, even double-deckers, were driven by women, who had to be quite brawny to handle the steering, which in those days was not, of course, power-assisted. There were conductors then, too, and I can see them now threading their way through crowded vehicles issuing tickets, with little help from the dim lights at night.

By early 1941 I had met Jack, Audrey's friend, Olive, and Leonard – all on leave at various times. I had already met Cyril, who was kept busy putting out fires. One weekend Audrey and I went to stay with Brenda and Alan at Horsford, just outside Norwich, and while we were there we watched from a safe distance an air raid on the city. Alan, though hospitable, had strict non-conformist views on drinking, so our visits to the local pub had to be made without his knowledge!

It was a two-hour bus journey from Ipswich to Norwich but on at least one occasion Mr Meadlarklan managed to borrow a car for me – a *Morris 8* saloon. My other means of travel for a long time was Audrey's bicycle which she had bought out of her pocket-money paying a shilling a week. I suppose it could be said that I commandeered it – at any rate, I took it over and used it, whenever circumstances allowed, to ride from Wickham Market to Needham Market and back – a round trip of about 25 miles.

There was, though, one evening when I was at Audrey's home without the bike and went to catch the last bus into Ipswich (10.30 pm) only to see it disappear up the road. I had no option but to set out on foot and had covered about twelve miles before being picked up in the early hours of the morning by the driver of a Post Office van for the remaining few miles to Wickham Market. Arriving long past the official time for being in camp, I climbed the iron railings surrounding part of *Glevering Hall* – not, I should add, for the first time! Those iron railings are still there.

In March 1941 I had a week's leave and this gave me the opportunity to take Audrey to Guildford to meet my family. I expect Audrey was a bit apprehensive, but she needn't have been, for everyone took to her from the start and in no time she felt, as I had done with the Meads, that she was one of the family. It was an experience for her in other ways too as until then she had not travelled very far from East Anglia.

During our stay I introduced her to the delights of *Henekeys* and the *Lion Hotel,* and it was during one of our evenings at the latter that I summoned up the courage to 'pop the question'. I was over the moon when I received an instant 'yes', but, as was the custom in those days – as it may be even now in some circles – it was necessary for me to get her father's consent to our engagement. Audrey wasn't then 21, of course.

Losing no time, I went to a public phone box in the *Lion* and put through a call to next-door neighbours in Needham Market (the Meads didn't have a phone at the time). Mr Mead was called. I don't think he was unduly surprised when he heard my suitably worded request. At any rate, he raised no objections, though there was a proviso that Audrey would remain at home to help her mother while the war lasted, and I was overjoyed to hear him give his consent. Audrey and I had a celebratory drink before returning to my mother, father and Una to break the news. They were as delighted as I was. Our wedding was fixed for Saturday 14th March 1942.

Our week in Surrey soon came to an end. Audrey was back home in Needham Market and I was with the 48th helping to tear up the roads in and around Wickham Market in my *Valentine* tank. Our activities went further afield when the regiment took part in battle exercises with other units of the 22nd Armoured Brigade. We would drive our tanks the few miles to the little railway station at Melton, on the outskirts of Woodbridge, where we loaded them on to 'flats' – wagons without sides or ends which allowed the tanks to be driven up a ramp at one end. The leading tank continued from flat to flat, easily bridging the gaps between them, and all the others of the squadron followed until a complete train-load of tracked vehicles was ready to move off.

*Audrey and me on Guildford Station
at the time of our engagement*

One such exercise took place in West Suffolk, where the tanks were driven off the flats in reverse order. When the exercise was over and the train was reloaded for the return to Wickham Market my tank just wouldn't start. A fitter (mechanic) worked on the engine to put things right, but by the time he'd got us going again the tank train had left. This meant that we would have to drive the tank from the barracks in Bury St Edmunds to *Glevering Hall* – a distance of at least 40 miles – and there was no A14 then! There were five of us in the crew and I was the tank commander, having by then been promoted to the rank of corporal.

Our route back took us through Stowmarket and the centre of Needham Market right past the door of 47 High Street! What a surprise it was for Audrey and others of the family who were at home to see the lumbering *Valentine* grind to a halt outside their front door and five men jump out! A very welcome cup of tea was soon produced, to be followed by more substantial refreshment before we continued on our journey. The tank, of course, drew quite a crowd of curious onlookers while it was parked outside the house.

Another exercise, in Haughley Park between Stowmarket and Bury St Edmunds, took place during a very hot spell in June 1941, and we were there on the very day of Kaye's marriage to Cyril. Again, no chance of leave, so this was another family wedding that I missed.

Early on Sunday mornings I used to attend Mass with a regimental colleague who was a Roman Catholic. Afterwards we would have a good breakfast (a change from Army food!) in the *White Horse Hotel* in the centre of Wickham Market. Sadly, the hotel is no longer in existence. I should perhaps explain that, though brought up in the Protestant Church, in 1938 I had been persuaded by a girl I was friendly with to receive instruction as a prelude to becoming a Catholic. I was in fact received into that church. Maybe I should be regarded as a maverick Christian. My 'flirtation' with the RC Church, in a practical sense, was brief, but my allegiance to the Christian faith has never wavered and I have always been happy to take part in worship in any of its churches, though for the past sixty years I have practised as an Anglican. In my AB64 (Army identification book) I was put down as 'C of E'.

The people of Wickham Market were very kind to us and we received many invitations to make us feel at home. In a cellar just off the village square the WVS (Women's Voluntary Service) opened up a little café for us. The house is still there and I wonder what goes on in the cellar now? There was a garage just round the corner on the Ipswich road and that was where, in the 1940s, we hosed down our tanks!

Another memory of the village relates to the chemist's shop. Brenda's daughter Margaret (now living in Bury) was born in February 1941 to be followed in April by Marjorie's first-born, Michael (now in Australia), and I went to that shop to buy presents to mark their arrival in the world. I chose baby hairbrushes, a pink one for Margaret and a blue one for Michael. Little things like that stay in the memory.

The winter of 1940-41 was, as I have mentioned, quite severe. We were still in our bell tents, sleeping on palliasses – straw mattresses which had to be emptied and refilled every week – and it was extremely cold, even with our greatcoats piled on top of the blankets (no sleeping bags then). If we kept a bucket of water in the tent overnight there was about an inch of ice in the morning. But we survived, and despite the uninteresting, and not very satisfying, food we mostly kept healthy – as did the rest of the population on strictly-controlled rations.

Exercises with the tanks continued locally. One day the squadron I was with was lined up on open ground between Campsea Ash and the coast for an official photograph to be taken.

Valentines of 'B' Squadron 48th Battalion Royal Tank Regiment ~ Suffolk, June 1941

I remember, too, how on more than one occasion we drove our *Valentines* right over the roundabout flower-beds on the old inner Ipswich by-pass (Valley Road etc.). This was done to prevent the road surface being damaged through the skewing of the tank tracks in the course of steering.

Frank Attridge was still in the regiment, though I didn't see so much of him as before. He was engaged to a girl from Winchelsea in Sussex and she came to Wickham Market to stay until their marriage.

Towards summer I was told by the CO that he was recommending me for a commission. That involved appearing before a panel of senior officers headed by the Brigadier. So one day I was taken to Brigade HQ – I think it was at Wetheringsett – for the interview. It didn't last very long and my replies to questions must have been satisfactory. When it ended the panel conferred while I kicked my heels in another room until I was recalled to be told that I had been selected. For me, then, it was relatively easy and straightforward, whereas for others in succeeding years as the war went on the selection procedure was different: candidates for commission had to appear before WOSBs (War Office Selection Boards), were subjected to tests and, before going to OCTUs (Officer Cadet Training Units), as I did, had to spend six weeks at pre-OCTUs.

Officer Training and Marriage

1941-1944

In September 1941 I left the 48th to join No.3 OCTU at Perham Down in Wiltshire for six months' training, not far from that part of Salisbury Plain where we had been the previous year. It was, of course, sad for me to have to leave Audrey and the Meads, and all my friends in the regiment, but I made the most of every opportunity to hasten back to Suffolk whenever weekend leave was granted. I also kept in touch with John Mumford when the 48th moved to Scotland. We maintained a correspondence which incorporated a secret code we had devised, so that I knew where he was. That, of course, was strictly forbidden! The 48th eventually moved to Africa and later to Italy, where my old friend Frank lost an eye during one of the tank battles. John survived the war unhurt.

At Perham Down we started off with a few weeks of 'square bashing', i.e. carrying out drills on the barrack square under the command of a somewhat fierce and loud-mouthed sergeant, who actually turned out to be quite a pleasant chap off duty. There followed intense periods of training in the mechanics and handling of tanks, wireless communication and radio-telephony procedure, and gunnery, for which we went to the RTR ranges at Lulworth Cove in Dorset. Then there were what we called 'schemes'. These were exercises using small wheeled vehicles – vans, really – which gave us experience in map reading, tactics and communicating by radio. We went all over the place, invariably meeting up at a pub or café. Other training came under the heading of 'TEWTs' – Tactical Exercises Without Troops.

The blitz was at its height towards the end of our days at Perham Down, and it was during one heavy night attack on London that many commercial buildings in the City area off Cheapside were destroyed by high explosive and fire bombs. One building that was hit housed my grandfather's business in Angel Court, Friday Street. Though contact with the firm's HQ in Switzerland had been cut off for some time my grandfather had just about managed to keep the British branch of the firm ticking over, but this was the end. With no hope of revival while the war continued there was no alternative for my grandfather but to retire. He was 74.

In the days leading up to our passing out we had been visited by London-based military tailors and measured up for our 'dress' uniforms (as opposed to the Army-supplied battle-dress which was our working uniform). To this were added such items as a Sam Browne belt, valise (bedroll), camp bed and canvas wash basin suspended on wooden legs. In other words, we were now kitted out as officers; we had already been allowed to wear khaki shirts of better quality than those issued, plus ties (at that time 'other ranks' did not wear ties).

By this time I knew that I wasn't going to be posted to a regiment, either at home or overseas. Instead, because I had done particularly well on the wireless course I was going as an instructor to the Wireless Wing of No.1 Pre-OCTU at Blackdown, not far from Aldershot.

* * * * *

So 12th March 1942 came and we all duly passed out. The next day, Friday the 13th (I don't think the significance of that crossed my mind at the time), we went our separate ways for a week's leave. For me it was to Ipswich, to the *Crown and Anchor Hotel* (now *W.H. Smiths*) where I met my father for what today is called a stag night. Rather a low-key one!

At OCTU in 1941-'42
I am standing in the centre of the back row

We stayed the night at the hotel and the next morning made our way by train to Stowmarket, where the Mead family, other relatives and a few friends of theirs, together with the Pyatts and Harrises – Mother, Una, Bunty and Arthur – were assembled at the church. It was a cold day but the sun shone for us and Audrey looked lovely in a dress which had been made for her sister Marjorie. Her bouquet was tied with ribbons in Royal Tank Regiment colours – brown, red and green, signifying 'Through mud and through blood to the green fields beyond.' It was a proud and deliriously happy moment for both of us.

Audrey's brother Jack was my best man. He had managed to get leave, and so had Marjorie's husband, Leonard, who travelled down from Scotland specially for the occasion. From the church we were all driven to 47 High Street, Needham Market for a reception at the Meads' home. It was a small-scale affair, as were most such occasions during the war, but a very happy one which enabled the two families to get to know each other.

At Stowmarket Parish Church
on 14th March 1942

The Wedding Party
My parents, Jack, me and Audrey, Audrey's parents and Anne

Ready to leave for our honeymoon!

After the reception, for us and for Leonard it was a taxi to Ipswich Station, where the three of us caught the train to London. It was ironic really that Leonard should be travelling with us, when I thought back to my father's honeymoon in 1922 and the crying little boy who insisted on going too! It was not quite the same though, for at Liverpool Street Leonard left us to go to another London terminus to catch a train back to Scotland, while Audrey and I got a taxi to the *Strand Palace Hotel*, where we stayed for a week.

Even in wartime blackout conditions London had its attractions, and we soon began sampling them. A favourite place was a basement pub in or off the Strand called, appropriately, the *Coal Hole*. We went to tea dances – popular then but, I suspect, unknown today – at Kingston, and visited relatives including my grandparents at Surbiton and a great aunt in the same area. The big London stores were functioning, so we made the rounds of those too.

That week went all too quickly. We returned to Needham on the Saturday and on the Sunday I left Audrey to join No.1 Pre-OCTU at Blackdown. There I found myself sharing a room with a Regular, Chris Gray, with whom I began a friendship lasting to this day. Our sleeping quarters were actually the court-martial room of the barracks. Among others in the Wireless Wing with Chris and myself were Geoff Goom, a Lyons tea-taster in Civvy Street, Raymond Thomson – better known by his stage and TV name of Raymond Francis – and Jack Medland.

The courses we ran comprised classwork covering wireless theory and RT (radio telephony) procedure as required for operational communication, and map reading. We used recording equipment (78-rpm) to familiarise our pupils with the use of the wireless transmitting sets they would be using in tanks. Employing a fleet of small vehicles, we devised 'schemes' on the lines of those I had taken part in at Perham Down to give our classes experience of map reading and communicating on the move. The wireless course formed only one part of Pre-OCTU training; there were also courses in gunnery and in the handling and maintenance of vehicles, as well as the inevitable drill. The six weeks of training were very concentrated.

Among the particularly interesting characters in one of the intakes for which I was responsible was Frank Owen. No, not the journalist of the same name I was with on the Wisbech *Standard* and later *The Birmingham Post*, but a nationally-known figure, also a journalist, who had been elected as a Liberal MP at a very early age and who had more recently been a London newspaper editor. He was then well into his thirties, whereas the majority of his fellow trainees were barely out of their teens, and it was a matter of some doubt whether he would be able to cope with the technicalities of radio. But he did and he duly passed out at the end of the course. However, as a commissioned officer he did not, I believe, serve for very long in an active Tank Regiment; instead his talent was utilised in the field of publicity, public relations and Service publications. I think he eventually edited an Army newspaper in the Far East.

* * * * *

I had not been at Blackdown very long before I found that married officers were allowed to live out, i.e. with their wives. This, of course, posed a difficult problem for me, bearing in mind the 'proviso' I had accepted before Audrey and I were married. I had fully expected to be posted overseas as soon as I was commissioned, and it did not occur to me that Audrey and I would be able to live together somewhere in the UK while I was still on active service. Now, the opportunity was too good to be missed, and I decided to face what I rightly suspected would be the wrath of my father-in-law and look for a place where Audrey and I could be together.

I found our first 'home' at Ash Vale, about three miles from Blackdown. It was a four-berth trailer caravan parked in the garden of a large house, Ingoldsby, in which lived the widow of an Army major who had served in Malta. Electric lighting was laid on, there was a sink and a Propane gas cooker, and the outside toilet of the house was available to us. The lady owner readily agreed to let us have the caravan for the next three months or so.

Audrey was 'over the moon' when I broke the good news to her. Her mother and father, especially her father, were very displeased – to put it mildly. I had agreed that Audrey would remain at home to help her mother for the remainder of the war, hadn't I? What did I think I was doing taking her away? Perhaps it was ungentlemanly of me and morally wrong, though in retrospect my father-in-law's condition was really quite unreasonable, but I stuck to my guns and off to Ash Vale we went. I was definitely in bad odour, but I'm happy to say that the estrangement – though it was hardly as bad as that – didn't last very long and Mr Mead and I resumed our very happy relationship. I have a suspicion that my father-in-law might have acted as I did had he been presented with similar circumstances as a young man.

So our first home was in a caravan, and idyllic it was too. I would leave each morning to cycle on Audrey's bike to the camp at Blackdown, and for the first time Audrey found herself leading a life of leisure, for she could rest for as long as she liked and there was little to do in the way of housework. In the evenings we would go for long walks, often along the towpath of the nearby canal, and stop off for a beer in the local pub. There were visits to Guildford, too – by bus, of course – and we had visitors. Kaye and Cyril came for a week, bringing Bernard, then 15, with them. Kaye and Cyril were able to sleep in the caravan while Bernard was provided with a bed in the house. I well remember our visits to the pub, where I introduced Bernard not only to beer (even though he was under age) but to the game of shove-ha'penny.

* * * * *

As autumn approached we decided to look for more substantial accommodation. Our caravan home was fine during the summer but with winter coming the warmth of a house was essential and we also felt that we would like to be nearer the barracks. On 11th September we said goodbye to *Ingoldsby* at Ash Vale and moved into *Holmwood*, a small semi-detached house at Blackdown. A week later we went back to Suffolk for the wedding of Audrey's brother Jack to Josephine (José) Clark, again at Stowmarket.

Happy as we were together we were not very happy with *Holmwood* itself or with its permanent residents, a Mr and Mrs Nettleton. The Nettletons were not the friendliest of couples, but at least they provided us with a roof over our heads.

After a while we began another round of house-hunting and early in December we rejoiced on leaving *Holmwood* to take up residence in a larger house, *Orchardleigh* in Beach Road, Frimley Green, between Ash Vale and Blackdown. The house was occupied by two middle-aged ladies, sisters I believe, and they let out part of the downstairs to a doctor who held his surgery there. We had a sitting-room on the ground floor and a bedroom above, and Audrey shared the kitchen with the two sisters. I don't remember where the bathroom was – we probably shared that, too.

Meanwhile my good friend John Mumford had been married in October 1942 to Doreen Taylor at Pembroke Dock. I'm happy to say that as I write these words in November 2001, John and Doreen, with whom I have exchanged Christmas cards over the many intervening years, are still together at Winchcombe near Cheltenham.

On 1st October 1942, I became a war substantive lieutenant. That was good news for us but there was bad news to come, for the 19th of that month was a terrible day for the people of Needham Market. A German sneak raider dropped two 500-pound bombs on the town centre, killing four people and injuring many others. Our wedding-day home, dear old 47 High Street, was blown to pieces. Fortunately for the Meadlarklans, they had moved in the summer to *Rose Villa*, a detached house further up the street on the outskirts of the town.

Early in December Jack went home for embarkation leave before setting off for Africa with his RASC unit, and on the 23rd of the month Audrey and I went back to Needham for a quiet but most enjoyable Christmas and New Year. We took Anne to Ipswich *Hippodrome* to see the pantomime *Cinderella*. On 2nd January we returned to Frimley Green, bringing Anne with us for three weeks' holiday. We put her up on a camp bed in our bedroom. During her stay I was laid up for a week with something akin to glandular fever, so it was left to Audrey to take her around, on foot or by bus.

One such trip she made was to Guildford to visit my parents and Bunty and Arthur, who by this time had a year-old daughter, Valerie. This visit is particularly remembered for the fact that, as we were short of fuel (coal was, of course very strictly rationed and we had no other means of heating), Audrey staggered home on the bus with Anne carrying two large bags of coal which my parents spared for us.

When Anne's holiday came to an end my father collected her and took her back to Suffolk by train, fitting the journey in with his business travels in East Anglia.

* * * * *

We had continued our search for better accommodation and by early February of 1943 we found it in *The Parsonage* at Frimley

Green, where we settled down happily for the next year. The house sits right next to the village church and was then the home of the vicar, the Rev Philip Isdell-Carpenter, and his young wife. They made us very welcome, providing us with a spacious and well-furnished lounge in which they had installed a small cooker, and a double bedroom upstairs. Within a few months, when we knew that Audrey was expecting a baby, a bedroom was set aside for a nursery and we had our own bathroom.

All in all the year passed very pleasantly in Frimley Green. The war dragged on and air raids were frequent, though by now the Allies were giving Germany a battering from the skies. Light was beginning to appear at the end of the tunnel with everyone, especially the Russians, becoming impatient for the opening of the long-awaited second front in the shape of an invasion of continental Europe. My work in the Wireless Wing at Blackdown continued. Each intake comprised some 30 cadets, so in the course of a year at least 600 must have passed through the hands of Chris Gray, Geoff Goom, Ray Francis, Jack Medland and myself.

Off duty we enjoyed the occasional social function in the officers' mess. Chris had a little *Morris Minor* then and usually took Audrey and me home after these events. He was still living in the barracks as he was not then married. We both had good friends among the officers and their wives. Sometimes we would go to the cinema in nearby Farnborough, and on one such occasion we bumped into an actor who had been a pre-war friend of Audrey's in Felixstowe.

I mentioned earlier that Frank Owen was one of my cadets. As we had a common interest in newspapers I invited him home to have supper with us one evening. Maybe that was 'politically incorrect', though that term was unknown then and in any case I am sure no-one bothered. Later, as a return gesture, Frank invited us to spend a short weekend with him and his wife at their luxurious flat in the Westminster area of London.

It was rather embarrassing for Audrey as our first-born was then well on the way – embarrassing in those days but it wouldn't be now, of course. Anyway, we were delighted to accept his invitation (even more 'politically incorrect', I suppose!) and duly went to London with Frank and another cadet – a member of one of the big brewing families – travelling in a hired limousine.

The Owens' beautiful and extensive flat was managed by a resident housekeeper and Frank's wife, an American oil magnate's heiress and herself a former beauty queen, gave us their own bedroom. I can see now the range of fitted wardrobes full of beautiful clothes and dozens of pairs of shoes.

For our evening out in the West End Audrey wore an elegant stole which Frank's wife insisted on her borrowing. Despite wartime food rationing, we dined very well at one of London's best restaurants before going to the theatre, where we had a box to watch that famous play, *Arsenic and Old Lace*. It was indeed a fantastic weekend for us at a time when one felt the benefit of such enjoyment amid the gloom of blackouts and war news.

* * * * *

And so the months of 1943 came and went. In about midsummer the Isdell-Carpenters had a son, and as September drew near we finalised preparations for the arrival of *our* first child. We had already booked a place for Audrey at *Mount Alvernia* nursing home in Guildford, where Valerie had been born in 1941. At that time the nursing home was run by nuns and the regime was very strict.

Early in the morning of Sunday 5th September, it was clear that the time had come for Audrey to go into the nursing home. Unfortunately for us, it happened to be my turn, as duty officer, to lead the regimental church parade. My appeal to the adjutant to be excused and replaced by another officer was in vain – I had to lead the church parade and that was that. Hurried inquiries followed and we had to thank the wife of a fellow officer (in peacetime he had been a county cricketer) for offering to go with Audrey in a taxi to Guildford – a journey of about 15 miles.

Ingoldsby
where we lived in a caravan in the garden – our first home.

Perhaps it was provident that, going to church, I was in the right place to say a prayer for Audrey, for all went well and, by the time I was able to go to Guildford later in the day, Stephen had been safely delivered. Audrey was fine but baby Stephen was born with jaundice and looked a poor little chap. Happily, he soon got well.

Almost certainly we spent another Christmas, 1943, at Needham, and as the new year of 1944 came the general feeling everywhere was that a crucial point in the war was fast approaching.

Stephen takes a bow!

By this time the Allies had long since won the war in North Africa and were winning more battles in Sicily and Italy. Those of us on the instruction staff at Blackdown realised that before long we would be posted to active units of the RTR, and such was indeed the case with Chris Gray, Geoff Goom, Jack Medland and myself – Raymond Francis was to stay on a little longer.

Chris, Geoff and I were summoned to London, where at his services' club we were interviewed by Lieutenant-Colonel Michael (Mike) Carver, commanding 1 RTR. The First – the senior tank regiment of the 7th Armoured Division, known as the Desert Rats – had lately returned to the UK from the fighting in Italy after their battles in the desert, and were being re-equipped with *Cromwell* tanks. The regiment was stationed for further training near Mundford in Norfolk, on the edge of Thetford Forest and not far from the Stanford battle area (years later the location for *Dad's Army* filming).

I don't think it took Mike Carver very long to size us up and decide that we were good enough to be appointed to the First. Chris and Geoff were both then unmarried, whereas I was not only married but a father. He didn't say so, of course, but I have always felt that Mike took that into account when choosing Chris and Geoff as troop officers, i.e. commanding a group of tanks within a squadron, and me as his signals officer, a job which carried less risk. Maybe I am wrong, but in the event I came through without a scratch whereas Chris lost an eye in one of the early battles in Normandy and Geoff lost his life in the battle for Caen.

The Invasion and the Battles in Normandy

1944

Early in 1944 there were farewells with our brother officers at Blackdown, most of whom were also posted to active units of the RTR, and at Frimley Green Audrey and I said goodbye to the Isdell-Carpenters. It was a sad day for us, and was in fact the last time we were to see them. They eventually moved to the Salisbury area and we kept in touch for many years. At one time they were kind enough to offer Audrey and Stephen a home while hostilities continued, and I know that Audrey always regretted that she did not take them up on it.

As it was I deposited Audrey and Stephen at the family home in Needham, where Marjorie and Michael were already installed, while I went on to join 1 RTR in the wilds of Mundford – not all that far away. There we were accommodated in Nissen huts.

As one would expect, the accent was very much on training, the new tanks being equipped with more powerful guns and an advanced radio communication system (No.19 sets). There was much to keep us occupied and we had very little free time. But, again discovering that living out was allowed, I started to spend what free time I did have cycling round the area on Audrey's bike, which I had collected from Needham and brought back on a train to Brandon, in search of accommodation. Luck was with me again. This time it was at *The Vicarage* in Brandon, where the Kirkpatricks proved as charming and helpful as the Isdell-Carpenters. We were provided with a bed-sitting-room and there was a small room adjoining for Stephen. Though Audrey cooked some meals for us she was often asked to join the family in the dining-room. And there, too, also in temporary residence, was our regimental chaplain.

The days were long for Audrey as I had to leave at about 6.30 am and cycle six miles to camp at Mundford and it was evening before I returned. I think Audrey got to know the small Suffolk town of Brandon quite well, pushing Stephen in his pram around its streets and squares.

Training was intense. Schemes (exercises) were made as realistic as possible and we covered a lot of ground in our new tanks. I ran wireless refresher courses for the radio operators and in those days this included the Morse code. Tank crews had to be at a peak of efficiency with their new vehicles, armament and communication system. Our No.19 wireless sets provided contact within the troop, squadron, brigade HQ and within the tank itself. Since I had been an instructor for two years, this aspect of training wasn't difficult for me, but don't ask me to do it now!

We knew, of course, that all this, including the living out, wasn't going to last very long and, sure enough, after about two months the order came for the regiment to move to Orwell Park on the outskirts of Ipswich (of all places for me!), with its beautiful grounds sweeping down to the river. The boys' school there had by then been evacuated to Shropshire but today it is back in Orwell Park as a co-educational school.

Audrey, then, was left at Brandon to fend for herself and little Stephen. But not quite, for those supremely kind people, the Kirkpatricks, not only helped her to the station to catch the train to Needham via Bury St Edmunds, but insisted on paying her fare. If that isn't a good example of the spirit that prevailed during the war, then I don't know what is. It was akin to the Isdell-Carpenters' offer to give Audrey and Stephen a home while the war lasted.

So 1 RTR, with other 22nd Armoured Brigade units of 7th Armoured Division, moved into Orwell Park, where we were again housed in Nissen huts. And it was in the grounds of the park that over a period of several days all our vehicles, tracked and wheeled, were waterproofed in readiness for the forthcoming landings on the Continent of Europe, though just where that would be we did not then know. Fifty-seven years later, in September 2001, a memorial tablet to our brief occupation of Orwell Park was unveiled in the grounds (I shall mention this later in my story).

It was from the park that the tanks of 1 RTR moved to Felixstowe for loading on to TLCs (tank landing craft). The regiment's wheeled vehicles went to the Port of London area to assemble at West Ham football stadium before being taken aboard 'liberty' ships (wartime pre-fabricated vessels built in the United States by a man named Henry Kaiser) for the voyage to ... wherever it was to be in Europe.

My own stay in Orwell Park was cut short, for I was responsible for a group of wheeled vehicles and had a Jeep for myself and my driver, a young man named Baer whose Jewish parents had fled from persecution in Germany in the '30s. We called him Max Baer after a famous boxer of that era.

I thought it was a 'bit much' having to leave the Ipswich area for West Ham! However, I did manage to see Audrey again before we set off for the D-Day operation. I borrowed an Army motor-cycle and rode it to Ipswich, where Audrey was waiting for me at her sister Kaye's flat (in a building opposite County Hall and now turned into a night club). The next day I sped back to West Ham, where for several days we were virtually incarcerated in the stadium.

* * * * *

It was in the early hours of D-Day itself that we set sail in our 'liberty' ships – at about the time that our advance forces were storming the Normandy beaches. By then we had been told that we were in fact going to Normandy, and later that day I was given a map reference so that (hopefully) I could lead my transport to wherever it was the tanks of 1 RTR had assembled. The planned landings had allowed for the tanks to go ashore first after the initial assault and for all the remaining vehicles and their crews to land at pre-determined intervals – otherwise there would have been chaos on the beaches. In the event the landings, so far as 1 RTR was concerned, were effected remarkably smoothly.

I remember the day – 6th June – well. As we sailed through the English Channel we were all lying around the deck of our ship, many of us whiling away the time reading books (extraordinary as that may seem) and the sun shone. Long-range guns opened fire on us from the French coast but I don't recall any hits, though there were several huge spouts of water as shells exploded in the sea around us.

It was very late in the afternoon when we dropped anchor some hundred yards or so off the beach at Arromanches (code named Gold), and there we were to remain until the morning of 8th June (D-plus 2). So we spent two nights on board. Around us were various other vessels, naval and transport, and both by day and by night big warships of the Royal Navy fired salvos over us to pound targets inland. It really was quite awe-inspiring seeing the flashes of the massive guns.

Although we had aerial superiority the Germans still had the capability of sending up bombers, often at night, in an attempt to disrupt the landings, and on both nights when we were on board our 'liberty' ship we were subjected to aerial attack. Two ships near us were hit yet somehow we escaped. I remember that my bed, such as it was, on the deck was just underneath a Bofors gun and the noise when it was being fired was deafening.

The time arrived for us to land and this was achieved by means of huge motorised rafts on to which all our vehicles were lowered and secured. When everyone was aboard, the rafts chugged slowly towards the beach until the depth of the water was about three feet, when each vehicle in turn was driven down a ramp into the sea and thence to the beach (thank goodness we had done our waterproofing properly!).

By the time we hit the beach, the section we were to use had been cleared of mines and marked out, so we knew where to go to reach the comparative safety of the hinterland through which we would have to go to join up with the rest of 1 RTR. All around us was evidence of the fighting that had taken place not many hours earlier. Houses fringing the beach were smoking ruins.

It did not take us long to find the rest of the regiment. HQ was in an orchard a mile or so from the town of Bayeux (home of the famous tapestry), which amazingly escaped major damage in spite of the ground fighting and bombing. The tanks were dispersed in neighbouring fields and orchards which provided some cover.

Now we were in France at last and the long drawn-out battle to end the war in Europe had begun. History books record in great detail the subsequent course of events as the Allied forces met increasingly strong opposition which penned us in the bridgehead for several weeks. The enemy had been caught by surprise by the area chosen for the landings, but lost no time in switching powerful Panzer divisions to the Normandy area, getting through despite being heavily bombed *en route*. Over the next few weeks we faced up to nine of these tank divisions, and fierce battles raged in the thickly hedged *bocage* country of Normandy during June and July, with heavy losses on both sides. Except for their speed and manoeuvrability our tanks were no match for the German *Royal Tigers*, equipped with more powerful guns, which the Germans dug in at strategic points. Often these heavy tanks could only be dislodged by RAF *Typhoon* dive bombers. The Germans' *Panthers*, though lighter than the *Tigers*, were also heavily armed.

Most of the villages were quickly reduced to ruins. I remember especially Villers-Bocage, where very little was left standing. The biggest battle so far as 7th Armoured was concerned was for the city of Caen. Paratroops from an armada of gliders had secured parts of the outlying area – we came across these gliders lying just as they had crash-landed – including a vital bridge, and the city was constantly under aerial attack from both US (by day) and RAF (by night) heavy bombers. But many days were to pass before the tremendously battered city was finally taken by the Allies.

In the meantime 1 RTR was frequently on the move in the relatively confined area of the bridgehead, suffering many casualties but also inflicting considerable damage on the enemy. Within about a fortnight our Commanding Officer, Lieutenant-Colonel Mike Carver, left us to take over a brigade, and about this time my friend Chris Gray was severely wounded, losing an eye, so was evacuated to England and no longer took part in the fighting in Europe. Our replacement CO didn't stay with us for very long, and he was succeeded by Lieutenant-Colonel Pat Hobart, a fine officer who led 1 RTR for the remainder of the war and on to Berlin.

By this time the famous Mulberry Harbour – in effect an artificial port – off the beachhead at Arromanches was being used to land reinforcements of men and materials. I went to the harbour for supplies on several occasions and a most impressive sight it was. Many years later Audrey and I went to Arromanches, and there we saw the remains of the harbour lying on the beach and sticking out of the sea. PLUTO (Pipeline Under The Ocean) was also in operation from D-Day onwards and that was how fuel reached us.

It was during the heaviest fighting for Caen that our trio in the First from Blackdown was reduced to one (me) through the death in battle of Geoff Goom. Although single when we were interviewed by Mike Carver, he had been married shortly before we set sail for Normandy, so poor Geoff's married life was short-lived – one of so many casualties. Two others remain fixed in my memory: two of our regiment's medical officers in succession were killed before the breakout from the bridgehead.

In the later stages of the battle for Caen I was with a column of trucks carrying fuel and ammunition on the slopes of fields, and had to take the column through the city to the front line on the other side. It was a night to be remembered. German bombers were in the sky that night so we took shelter in a railway station goods yard close to the Orne Canal. How the enemy missed us I shall never know, but they did, dropping their bombs all around us, most falling into the canal. As dawn approached we made our getaway from the station and succeeded in reaching and replenishing our tanks. While there I watched a *Typhoon* dive-bombing a dug-in *Royal Tiger* which was proving a nuisance.

On the lighter side of our days in Normandy one of my memories is of the complete absence of bread for at least six weeks. You don't realise how much you would miss it until it happens to you! Army biscuits, on which we had to depend, were no substitute. But we did manage to get hold of some locally-produced food from time to time, including eggs, from those farms or smallholdings which were still functioning. Generally the people of Normandy were not then over-friendly, which is perhaps understandable considering that, while being thankful to be liberated, they were not exactly happy about the war being fought on their doorstep, and I suspect they were mighty glad when the fighting moved on.

The Sweep across France into the Low Countries and Germany

1944-1945

With the eventual capture of Caen and the closing of the Falaise Gap to the south, the Allies made a sweep across France, on into Belgium and then into Holland, before the big drive ground to a halt. In contrast to our days in the Normandy beach-head when we moved about in a confined area, now we made long drives from area to area, dealing effectively with German opposition on the way. This was the time when we were capturing and destroying the sites from which the enemy had been launching V1 'doodle-bugs' and V2 rockets from Northern France on Southern Britain's cities and towns, causing many casualties.

The 'doodle-bugs', small crewless aircraft packed with explosives, were bad enough but at least they could be heard coming and, taking what cover they could, people knew that when the engine cut out the craft would plunge to the ground and explode. The V2s were different, being rocket-propelled missiles which gave no audible warning of their approach: they just hit the ground and exploded before anyone knew what was happening. So it was a great relief for the population of Southern England when the last of the sites from which the V1s and V2s had been launched was put out of action. The V2s, incidentally, were the forerunners of the space rockets developed by the Russians and Americans after the war.

In the course of our drive across France there was an occasion when I was with our supply vehicles leaguered up in a large field, the camouflaged trucks tucked alongside hedges, as our forward-placed tanks were engaging the enemy, and a German prisoner was passed back to us. A pleasant young chap, he showed us photos of his family and we gave him cigarettes, assuring him that he would be safe and well treated when we in turn passed him further back to another British unit which handled prisoners. Most unfortunately, however, he decided to make a run for it; either he feared for his life in our hands, despite our assurances, or he was determined to get back to his own side. The poor chap sprinted across the field, and as we could not let him get away, because he would be in a position to pass on details of our strength and position, he had to be stopped. Ignoring our shouts he raced on... until someone aimed his rifle and fired. The young German dropped like a stone, the bullet having gone right through his head. We all felt so sad about this.

Some of the places we stopped in, passed through or by-passed as we continued our way across Northern France were Lisieux, Rouen, Amiens, Bethune and Lille, and in Belgium, Ghent, Antwerp and Brussels. The Guards Armoured Division had actually captured Brussels while we were some miles to the north, but I did get to the Belgian capital soon after its liberation when, with three other officers from the regiment, I was given 48 hours' leave – a welcome respite, as one can imagine. We made the most of our time in the city, where we stayed in one of the leading hotels and slept in huge beds complete with real sheets and duvets. How did we get to Brussels and back to the regiment? In a comfortable requisitioned civilian car!

For a time my Jeep was replaced by a 15cwt truck, which proved very useful as sleeping quarters – as opposed to a trench in the ground! An officer with whom I became friendly was

'Judge' Henson, so called because in civilian life he was a solicitor. He and I often played cards in the truck at night when it was 'all quiet on the front'.

From Belgium we moved on into Holland, the land of dykes and bridges. Tilburg and Eindhoven were taken, the latter being the home of the huge *Philips* electrical concern, from which we acquired very useful hand-operated batteryless torches. Another town captured by the 7th Armoured was s'Hertogenbosch.

The vital objective in Holland was to secure the bridges spanning the Rhine. For the British the main target was the bridge at Arnhem. Once in command of this the 2nd Army was to turn the German flank and rapidly assault the Ruhr through the 'back door' into Germany. That was the plan and on 17th September the largest airborne and glider operation ever mounted took place. More than 5,000 aircraft were involved.

The landings went well but, partly because Allied intelligence had disregarded Dutch underground reports that a German Panzer corps was in waiting outside Arnhem, the resistance encountered was far greater than had been bargained for, and only one parachute battalion actually managed to reach the bridge. The bravery of this heavily outnumbered British force is history and was depicted in the film, *A Bridge Too Far*. The rest of the division was pinned down in and around the town, so this daring operation failed.

Of the 10,300 men who landed at Arnhem, 1,300 were killed and more than 6,400 captured. Just 2,587 managed to escape, and among them was my sister-in-law Greta's husband, Dennis Cutting. Dennis had been dropped by parachute; 50 years later he returned to Arnhem for commemorative celebrations and made another jump at the age of 70 – this time in tandem.

The original plan had been for 30 Corps, which included 1 RTR, to relieve the airborne troops and carry the offensive forward. But we were delayed by German resistance and congestion along the narrow corridor to Arnhem. So with the failure to take the bridge our advance came to a halt. It was frustrating, to say the least, to be held up at such a vital time when so much had been gained.

I recall one day when I was with supply vehicles on the flat open ground of a farm and an intense attack was launched by the Germans. We quickly scurried for cover – I was actually out in the open cleaning my teeth when the firing began – and crouched in pig-sties while the attack lasted. Fortunately we suffered no casualties but some of our trucks were set on fire.

With the Allies poised on the fringes of Germany, but the northern thrust having come to nothing because of the failure at Arnhem, stalemate set in along the entire front for several weeks. Then Hitler made a last-ditch attempt to split the Allied armies by launching a strong lightning thrust through the Ardennes aimed at Antwerp. The Battle of the Bulge began on 16th December and Monty was given command of all Allied forces north of the penetration. The Americans bore the brunt of the German attack, and it was their gallantry – and a shortage of petrol suffered by the Germans – that brought the offensive to an end by mid-January of 1945.

By then the Allies were ready with the largest military force ever assembled to advance on Germany. Nearly four million American, British and Canadian troops were engaged in the last offensive to finish off Nazi Germany, while from the east the Russians were closing in on Berlin.

We had spent Christmas in a place called Geleen near Sittard, situated on a narrow neck of Holland between Belgium and Germany. It was very cold and thick snow lay on the ground. My Jeep driver and I found a billet in the home of a friendly family. We slept indoors but cooked our own meals in the street. There were two little boys in the family, one having the (to me) curious name of Hoopie; today they would be in their sixties. Their father was manager of a nearby coal mine.

For all of us it was a very different Christmas from what we had been used to and our thoughts were much about our families at home. Audrey and Stephen were at *Rose Villa* in Needham Market along with Marjorie and Michael, Anne, Bernard and my parents-in-law.

Over the many months since I had last seen Audrey in Ipswich we had kept up a regular correspondence (via the Army post office). I say regular, but the arrival of letters was necessarily spasmodic and sometimes I would get half a dozen letters from Audrey at one time, and she did likewise. I often wrote at least three letters a day! That may seem extraordinary in battle conditions, but there were lulls when we kicked our heels and had to find something to do – which didn't take me long!

For security reasons all letters were subjected to censorship, and it fell to me to check the correspondence of the 'other ranks' in my charge. This was not a pleasant task and I did my best to skate over particularly personal passages. My own letters were scanned by more senior officers.

It was when we were in the Sittard area that the regiment was allocated a place for an officer on a wireless course at the RTR's HQ in Dorset. I'm sure that I didn't really need to spend six weeks on a refresher course, but the colonel evidently thought I did – or felt that I had earned a break. At any rate he decided that I should go to Bovington and by various means that is where I went about mid-January 1945. It was a Heaven-sent opportunity to see Audrey and Stephen and even, as it turned out, to be in England when Andrew was born.

During the course I was able to pay flying visits to Needham at weekends. One Saturday I received a telegram to tell me that Andrew had arrived and I was soon off to catch the first train to

London and thence to Suffolk. I was met by Marjorie who told me that, as Audrey was resting after a somewhat fraught night, I ought to wait until the evening before going to the *Allington* nursing home in Ipswich to see her and our new baby.

From Marjorie I learnt of the night's events. Audrey had gone into labour very late on the Friday night and the family's next-door taxi-driver had been summoned well after midnight. By the time they reached the *Allington*, Andrew had very nearly made an early appearance and it was all the taxi-driver and Marjorie could do to keep him in check until the doorway of the home was reached. Within minutes Andrew was safely delivered, all was well with Audrey and the baby and the taxi departed for Needham with an exhausted Marjorie in the back.

I was able to see Audrey more than once over that weekend, and later, when the course at Bovington was finished, I had a short leave before returning to the battle front.

* * * * *

In my innocence I thought there would be little difficulty in finding my way to wherever 1 RTR was, so long as I was given a map reference and other directions when I reached Belgium. How wrong I was! At the transit camp I was told that I would have to wait while a decision was made about which regiment I was to be posted to – presumably as a troop officer in a unit which needed a replacement. No way was I going to accept this without a protest and I emphasised how important it was for 1 RTR to have its own signals and transport officer back. To my relief it was eventually agreed that I should return to my own regiment.

By this time 1 RTR had already crossed the Rhine, and within a few days I managed to catch up with the regiment and was back in harness, as it were. Over the next two or three months the Allied armies pressed on in the general direction of Berlin and by the end of April 1 RTR and other elements of 7th Armoured Division were outside Hamburg, in the area of Harburg on the River Elbe, poised to launch a full-scale attack on the city. German resistance was now crumbling all along the extensive Allied front. The end of the war in Europe was very near and, though we did not know it at the time, Montgomery was about to meet enemy commanders on Luneburg Heath on 4th May to accept the surrender of all German forces in the north.

Posing in front of the Jeep which I drove across France and the Low-Countries to Berlin

So we literally sailed into and through Hamburg, which surrendered to us on 3rd May, coming to rest between the ruined city and the Kiel Canal and a small town near Itzehoe. There, on VE-Day we raised the Union Jack on our lead tank, and with the war over, we knew we wouldn't be pressing on to liberate Denmark as expected.

The war in Europe formally ended on 8th May 1945, when the Germans surrendered unconditionally at Reims in France.

At the end of the line

When hostilities ceased I was stationed in a village near Meldorf, where it was my duty to give certain orders to the villagers. The notice overleaf was issued and signed by me and stuck up on noticeboards around the village.

```
                    P R O C L A M A T I O N.

1.   Alle Anfragen werden an den Bürgermeister gestellt.

2.   Zivilisten dürfen 5 Kilometer von BERGENSTEDT gehen
     sowie nach MELDORF, ohne Bescheinigung.   In keinem
     Fall wird Erlaubnis gegeben diese Grenzen zu
     überschreiten.

3.   Fahrräder dürfen benutzt werden; aber sollten die
     angelegten Grenzen überschritten werden, werden alle
     Fahrräder eingezogen.

4.   Alle Fragen wegen Lebensmittel, Wohnschaften u.s.w.
     werden von dem Bürger meister behandelt.

5.   Deutsche Soldaten in diesem Dorf, werden bald von
     einem Deutschen Kommandant Ihre Befehle bekommen.
     Momentan müssen Sie bleiben wo Sie sind und dürfen
     Ihre Landarbeit fortsetzen.

6.   Vorrübergehend sind alle Deutsche Soldaten in diesem
     Dorf unter der Leitung von Ober-Leutnant STRASSER.

                                              Lt.
     16 May 45.                    OVC., A2 Echelon,
                                   1st R.T.R.
```

1. All enquiries are to be directed to the Mayor.

2. Civilians may travel up to 5 kms from Bergenstedt as well as
    to Meldorf without a permit.   In no case will permission be
    given to go beyond these boundaries.

3. Bicycles are allowed but should the boundaries be exceeded all
    cycles will be confiscated.

4. All enquiries abut food, property etc. will be dealt with by the
    Mayor.

5. German soldiers in this village will soon receive their orders
    from a German Commander.   At present you must remain
    where you are and may continue your agricultural work.

6. All German soldiers are temporarily under the command of
    Lieutenant Strasser.

We remained in the Itzehoe area for several weeks until, in late August, the regiment was ordered to Berlin, which had been taken by the Russians. So we were now going to reach the end of the line after six years of war.

I think I am right in saying that of the original officers of the regiment who set out from England on 6th June 1944, just two, the quartermaster and myself, made it to Berlin. The rest had either been killed, evacuated as casualties or transferred to other units and replaced by new faces.

* * * * *

We then left the Hamburg area and the entire regiment made its way through Russian-occupied territory along the autobahn (motorway) from Helmstedt to the much-devastated German capital. This was the one and only route to Berlin for traffic from the West and the Russians were very careful to see that we didn't stray from it.

Arriving in Berlin, we made our way through the city to the former Luftwaffe base at Kladow Barracks close to the Van Zee (a lake), and it was in the barracks there that I spent the remainder of my days in the Army. The officers' quarters were quite comfortable, even luxurious to us after more than a year living rough.

By this time 1 RTR had been re-equipped with new tanks, *Comets* replacing the battle-worn *Cromwells*. Training and the re-emergence of 'spit and polish' kept us occupied, and off duty there were forays into the city. A lot of clearing up had been done, but in the main streets there were still huge piles of rubble alongside the shattered buildings. It would be a long time before life for the inhabitants returned to anything like normal. There were shortages of everything and food was basic; about the best that could be offered in the few restaurants still open was cabbage and potatoes. The famous Tiergarten was the scene of much unofficial bartering of black market goods.

127

By agreement between the Allies the city had been divided into four sectors – Russian, British, American and French. With some difficulty we used to make our way through check-points into the Russian sector, though there was little to be had there and we weren't particularly welcome. Hitler's Chancellery building – or what was left of it – was in the Russian sector and I did manage to get inside it to rummage round. But there were no souvenirs to be found – the Russians, getting there first, had seen to that.

I remember going to the Opera House one Sunday and seeing Beethoven's *Fidelio* – a somewhat sombre opera. I also went to the Olympic Stadium where Hitler used to address the massed ranks of his cohorts.

At this time Audrey's younger brother, Bernard, was now in the Army, having been called up in the later stages of the war. He was also serving in Germany and by some means or other I heard that he was going to be in Berlin for a few days. How we managed to get in touch I cannot recall, but we arranged to meet in the city. It was a very pleasant change for both of us to be together for a few hours – a mini family reunion.

Two other events during my seven months in Berlin loom large in memory: Field-Marshall Lord Montgomery's visit to 1 RTR and an eerie train journey that I made taking some 600 sick and wounded German prisoners (of the Russians) from Spandau, the Berlin suburb where Rudolf Hess was held in prison for many years, to Hannover in Western Germany.

Monty's visit was to mark his becoming Colonel Commandant of the Royal Tank Regiment and it took place on 20th September 1945. We spent days preparing for it: our new tanks and every other piece of equipment were cleaned and polished to the 'nth' degree and rehearsals were held to ensure that on the day of Monty's inspection and drive past everything would go according to plan.

To provide entertainment at a special concert for the troops Ivy Benson's Girls' Band was flown out from England. Ivy and her girls were put up at the nearby officers' club beside the Van Zee, where we spent pleasant hours with them, and where on other occasions I was given ballroom dancing lessons by a member of the WRVS.

Monty stayed in a large house in the grounds at Kladow, and it fell to my lot to be the officer in charge of the guard on one of the nights he was there. Guards patrolled the wooded area around the house, and behind the trees at various points there were alarm buttons.

Though the great man dined with us he didn't linger after the meal. A teetotaller and non-smoker, he left us to carry on celebrating and retired early to bed as he always did, even on the eve of a great battle.

The next day there was the most impressive line-up of *Comets* on the barracks square and when Monty had completed his inspection there followed a drive past at which he took the salute.

My lasting memory of Monty is of the penetrating look he gave me when he shook my hand. I don't mean that it was an unfriendly look – far from it – but it was the steely gaze of a man of strength who, you knew, could quickly size you up. The celebrations continued long after Monty's departure. He had far more important things to do.

* * * * *

A Handshake from Monty – I am fifth in line

Now for that train journey. The Russians held many thousands of German troops in POW camps and with the war now over the sooner the less able of them were returned to Germany the better – for both the Russians and the Germans. The fitter POWs were, I'm sure, held back to work for the Russians.

Many of the prisoners came from Western Germany and it was they who were brought to Berlin and handed over to the Western occupying forces for onward transit to their homes. Over a period of weeks 1 RTR was made responsible for several such trainloads and in due course it was my turn to gather a small group of NCOs and troopers to take charge of a batch of 600 German soldiers assembled at Spandau for the final leg of their journey homeward.

The train itself consisted of a large number of open wagons with a couple of covered wagons at the rear, and was drawn by a steam engine. The Germans embarked, and a sorry lot they were, too. They looked half-starved and nearly all of them were suffering from dysentery. We were provided with just enough basic food for them, and water of course, but whereas we British had the benefit of the covered wagons – in one of them I had my camp bed – the ex-prisoners had to make do with the open ones without any creature comforts.

We eventually set off, with documents authorising our passage through the Russian zone – and a fat lot of good these sometimes proved to be! It was anything but a pleasant journey and, instead of taking just a few hours at the most, it lasted for two days. It would have been slow enough anyway in view of the war-damaged state of the track and the hastily-repaired bridges – barely safe, I suspect, for the loaded train to pass over – but the principal cause of the constant delays, even frequent halts for hours on end, was the suspicions of the Russians. It seemed that our journey had to be authorised and re-authorised almost by the hour through telephonic communication with higher powers back in Berlin.

I remember that we spent the best part of a day in the station at Magdeburg while a particularly officious female colonel not only examined our papers several times but made many phone calls to her superiors before permitting the train to continue on its way. At another station trigger-happy young Russian soldiers fired off bursts with their sub-machine guns into the air or at tin can targets they had set up.

The journey was especially miserable for the poor Germans, herded into the wagons with little if any bedding and, of course, no toilets. Consequently, at the many unscheduled stops just about every one of the 600 would hastily leave the train to attend to the needs of nature alongside the track. Just imagine it!

That was bad enough. What was far more worrying for me was the discovery quite early on that we had on board 'stowaways' in the shape of a couple of female German nurses. Guessing what might well be their fate if they were to be discovered by the Russians, we had to devise ways in which these girls could be hidden when the train was halted and searched – as it often was. By one means or another, such as getting them to cling on to one side of our covered wagons while the Russian troops searched the other, we succeeded in keeping their presence a secret and safely delivered them to the British, along with the ex-prisoners, when we reached Hannover. Our journey was over, and the return to Berlin in the empty train proved uneventful.

With the approach of Christmas (1945) more changes were taking place within 1 RTR as, in ones and twos, officers, NCOs and other ranks left for demobilisation. Throughout the services this was carried out by placing everyone in numbered groups. Mine was 23 group and for reasons which I cannot recall the release of those in this group was delayed for a month or so. I was in fact given the opportunity of staying on for an unspecified longer period, but after more than six years in uniform I wanted to get back to Audrey and my young family as soon as I could. There was my career as a journalist to consider, too.

The Insignia of the Desert Rats

Back to Civvy Street

1946

Christmas came and went – I have no special memory of it – and we were now in 1946, the first full year of peace since 1938. My departure was due towards the end of January but there was a hitch – I went down with 'flu which delayed it for another week or so.

It was actually in February that I left 1 RTR and Berlin by train for Ostend, and in the transit camp there, who should I bump into but my friend and Blackdown colleague, Raymond Francis, who was running a theatre for the troops. We spent a pleasant hour together before I embarked for the sea crossing to Dover, and thence by train to the demob centre at Northampton. It was about 35 years later that Raymond and I met again at a former Wireless Wing reunion at Thame in Oxfordshire, by which time he had long been nationally known for his stage and television appearances as Inspector Lockhart in *No Hiding Place*. Regretfully I have to say that he has since died.

An uneventful journey to Northampton culminated in my joining a queue to be 'signed off' and issued with civilian clothing – suit, overcoat, hat and so on. What an anticlimax to my military career! Then it was on in another train to London and a third to Suffolk and a very happy family reunion at Needham Market.

In the months that immediately followed the end of the war in Europe I had taken a correspondence refresher course in reporting and sub-editing arranged by the National Union of Journalists. My work was overseen by a tutor in Oxford, and I also took the opportunity to brush up my shorthand. During one of the two leaves I had had in England I managed to get myself an interview with the press baron Lord Rothermere, whose *Daily Mail* group also owned provincial newspapers, including the *Evening Express & Echo* at Exeter. After my years on weeklies it had been my ambition to join a daily paper, and Exeter, which I had visited so many times as a boy, attracted me as a city and seemed a suitable place for my re-entry into journalism.

Evidently Lord Rothermere decided that I had something going for me as he said he would write to the editor of the *E & E* and that I should do the same. The upshot was that, without a further interview and on the strength of my letter and Lord Rothermere's approval, I was engaged as a reporter on the Exeter evening, the *Express & Echo*.

After a short spell of leave with Audrey, the boys and the Meads, I set off on my own for Exeter. It was really a repeat of my starting in Guildford ten years earlier for I stayed with my Uncle Willie and Aunt Marion at their house on Cowick Hill for the first week or so. This time, of course, I had to find a home, not just for myself but for a young family. This was no easy task, for Exeter had been damaged by bombing, so housing was in very short supply and, quite rightly, priority was given to ex-servicemen who came from the area. However, I managed to find a furnished house to rent in Ladysmith Road, Exeter.

It was an Edwardian terraced house with three bedrooms and the minimum of essential furniture. The kitchen cooker was thick with grease and the beds were home to numerous bugs. The asking rent was £3-0s 0d a week, but when the lady owner learnt that I had two young children she put that up to £3-10s 0d (£3.50), which made a big hole in my weekly pay of £6-7s 6d (£6.37½) – less deductions!

We really had no choice but to accept the offer of this house for we were determined to be together in our own home, so I journeyed back to Needham to collect Audrey, Stephen (then 2½), Andrew (just a year old) and our few belongings.

Ladysmith Road, Exeter in 1946

In March 1946 we began our peacetime life together as a family – a very happy family, too, I might add. And there was compensation for the gloomy house in the presence of very friendly and helpful next-door neighbours, as well as having my aunt and uncle not too far away in the city.

I soon took up the threads of reporting, covering union conferences, the usual round of events and courts, and some of Exeter city's football matches. We explored the surrounding area whenever we could, and at weekends, if I was free, we went by train to the beaches at Dawlish and Exmouth. On one occasion Stephen and I over-dosed ourselves with sunshine, the result being that we were both extremely burnt and had to go to the doctor; it was several days before I could bear to wear a jacket.

I spent one day in the summer in the town of Honiton, reporting the victory celebrations there, so Audrey and the boys were on their own at home as they also were on many evenings when I was working. Audrey was understandably nervous about being on her own with the children after dark, and I would arrive home, usually on a bike, to find all the lights in the house blazing forth from uncurtained windows. One evening at about midnight, when I was walking home pushing the bike with my portable typewriter balanced on the handlebar, I was stopped by a policeman who quite thought that he had apprehended a thief! Producing my union membership card, I was able to persuade him that I was merely a reporter with the 'tool' of my trade who had been working late.

It was a happy day, especially for Audrey, when the editor called me into his office and asked if I would like to be a sub-editor. Would I! Apart from the fact that it would be advancing my career – although little extra money was involved at the time – it would mean regular hours and no work at nights or on Sundays, so we could better enjoy family life.

As time went on that summer it became more and more obvious that we couldn't continue paying that £3-10s 0d rent indefinitely; as it was we had had to dip into our somewhat meagre savings (for my six years in the Army I had received a gratuity of £70), and the chance of finding a cheaper place or a council prefab were virtually nil. So we decided that I would contact the *East Anglian Daily Times* company in Ipswich to see whether there was a vacancy there for a sub-editor. If we went back to Suffolk we would initially move in with Audrey's parents – yet again!

I wrote to the *EADT* and back came a letter from the managing director-cum-managing editor, Ralph Wilson, asking me to attend for an interview at the company's London office in Fleet Street. On my day off I caught an Exeter-Waterloo train and duly found myself in a small office confronted by a large man who looked like a farmer and talked about everything except newspapers!

Ralph Wilson <u>was</u> the *Anglian* at that time, and for many years to come. Through family connections he had been through every department and there wasn't a job on the papers that he couldn't do. A charming and kind man, he was also odd in many ways and had the reputation of being quite a character.

The upshot of my interview – during which he did eventually come round to discussing the job – was that a week or so later (he liked to keep people waiting!) I received a letter appointing me a sub-editor on the *Evening Star*.

We had grown to like Exeter and I was very happy on the Express *& Echo*, but there was really no choice. The editor went so far as to offer me a rise but even that would have been insufficient for our needs. So, with some reluctance, I had to refuse his offer and start to make plans for our move back to Suffolk. We had taken the Ladysmith Road house on a six-month lease, which to me meant that at the end of five months I could give a month's notice to terminate the contract. But that wasn't how the landlady saw it – she maintained that we had to complete the six months and then give notice, and she demanded a further month's rent. I sought the advice of the newspaper's solicitor and he very kindly agreed to act for me, without payment, by sending a stiff letter to the landlady, if in return I would perform a service for him – carry out a search of the paper's files to find some information that he required. It worked – the landlady caved in, I found the information and all was well for us to leave Exeter on the date planned, a little over six months since we'd arrived.

Looking back, I realise it was asking a lot of Audrey's family to expect them to take us in again – for an unspecified length of time, too – but their kindness knew no bounds and the four of us were welcomed back into the household.

Our Family Grows – Work on the Evening Star

1946-1953

At the old *EADT* building (long since demolished) in Carr Street, Ipswich, I joined Alf Bowden ('Bow'), the chief sub-editor of the *Star*, Harry Holt, who had recently joined the staff from Yorkshire, and Walter Last, a much older man whose sole job was to handle all the horse racing news. That was the entire subs' room – a small team! Sport, other than the racing, was handled by an equally small team led by the sports editor, John Leathley. There was then no editor as such for the *Star*, and the morning *Anglian* was edited by Ralph Wilson himself, with its own team of night sub-editors. The sports staff covered for both dailies.

Bow was a journalist of the old school. He'd been a senior reporter before the war and his greatest scoop, of which he was justly proud, was to beat the National Press by breaking the news of the discovery of the burial site of an Anglo-Saxon ship and other artefacts at Sutton Hoo, beside the River Deben at Woodbridge. During the war he ran the *Star* single-handed. But he wasn't the kind of journalist to move with the times off his own bat, hence the recruiting of younger men, Harry Holt and myself, to breathe new life into the paper. And this we did, without any objection from Bow, though our efforts may appear rather dated today.

For the next seven years Bow, Harry and I, with Walter Last handling the racing news and John Leathley and his team looking after the sport, brought out the *Star* each day, working together very happily and handling reports of the many changes that were taking place in and around Ipswich in those immediate post-war years. The paper grew in size (more pages) as newsprint rationing eased, and circulation rose. In those days there was far greater dependence on newspapers for news of the day – television had hardly got restarted and even radio didn't pump out bulletins on the scale of today. The *Star* sold on the streets like hot cakes, and with much later deadlines than there are now we could print reports of events that took place far into the afternoon – court cases for example, and even the afternoon Question Time in the House of Commons. Our last edition, the Late Final, rolled off the press at 5.30 pm.

One of the big stories of the late '40s and early '50s concerned government proposals to include Ipswich in an expanded towns programme. A town planning expert, a professor whose name I have forgotten, drew up a plan for Ipswich which even included an overhead throughway which would have taken traffic from the Norwich Road through the centre of the town to the Felixstowe road. But it was not to be: other towns, such as Northampton, were expanded but Ipswich was left to develop in its own way.

Around the time I joined the *Star*, in September 1946, Ipswich appointed a new Chief Constable, James Crawford. Suffolk then had three separate police forces – for East Suffolk, West Suffolk and Ipswich – whereas today there is only one, and James Crawford was the youngest Chief Constable in the country. He died in 1981, a few years after his retirement. Today I am living in Waldringfield only a few yards away from his widow, Emily, who at the time of writing is 94 and one of the oldest residents in the village.

Opposite the printing works in Little Colman Street (since absorbed into the Carr Street shopping precinct) a couple of terraced houses had been converted into a social club for *EADT* employees. There, among other visitors, one would often find that great cartoonist Giles. He lived at Witnesham, a few miles outside the town, and had a studio in a building on the corner of the junction of the Buttermarket and Princes Street. Standing on the wide pavement on this corner today there is a memorial to Giles in the form of one of his best known characters – Grandma. During his working days Giles took his cartoons to Ipswich Station, where they were put on the train for London and the *Daily Express*.

I went to work each day on a bus from Needham Market with Mr Meadlarklan, who was the secretary of a wholesale grocery company in Museum Street. This went on for some six months until, in March 1947, I found a place of our own in Langer Road, Felixstowe, a small terraced house owned by a spinster who worked as a housekeeper for a farmer near Woodbridge.

The house was sparsely furnished and the amenities were quite basic, but it was clean. We were allowed to use only part of the house – to wit, the living room with an old fashioned coal fire; a kitchen with a stone sink, a cold water tap and an ancient gas-stove; two bedrooms and a loo outside in the yard. There was no hot water system and no bathroom; we heated water in a bucket on the gas stove and washed in a bowl or in a tin bath placed on the kitchen floor. The front room was out of bounds but a third bedroom could be used, for a small addition to the rent, if we had anyone to stay.

In retrospect it doesn't sound very enticing; in fact, we were all supremely happy in that little house. And we even managed – goodness knows how – to have my sister Bunty with Arthur and their two children to stay for a fortnight's holiday! My mother came to stay, too, when she was recuperating after an illness.

At the time Audrey's brother Jack was living in the Walton area of Felixstowe with José, and as Leonard was in the RAF, at the base where the docks are now, he and Marjorie were living in married quarters with their children Michael and Mary.

Michael went to Langer Road Primary School and it was there that Stephen, too, started his education.

Our days at Felixstowe passed very pleasantly, the promenade and the beach being almost on our doorstep, which was fine for the boys.

I caught the bus into Ipswich at eight o'clock each morning and would be home by 6.00 pm, except on Saturdays when, with the last edition of the *Star* printed, Bow, Harry and I continued working on the *Green 'Un*, our sports paper, which came out later.

We had moved into the Langer Road house in March 1947, and although I had our name on local housing lists, time went by with little sign that we qualified for a place of our own. By March 1949, however, we knew that our third child was on the way, so one day I decided to go yet again to the housing department in Ipswich to see whether anything could be done for us. I could hardly believe it when an official told me that I had made my latest approach at just the right time as a tenant was being sought for one of a block of four new houses fitted with experimental central heating, and this tenant would have to be a responsible person who would undertake to co-operate with the council and with *Cranes*, the engineering firm which had installed the heating, in keeping a check on the system. As I appeared to fit the bill, we were allocated the house and moved in almost straightaway.

* * * * *

Our new house was in Donegal Road, on the White House estate at Whitton, lying on the northern outskirts of Ipswich, and to us it was like moving into the *Ritz*. Brand new, it had a sitting room, dining room, kitchen with solid fuel boiler, and a brick-built outhouse/shed area with a toilet. Upstairs were three bedrooms – all with built-in wardrobes – and a bathroom with toilet. There were front and rear gardens and the neighbours were friendly. The tenants of two of the four houses were, by arrangement with the council, *Crane*'s employees who had been on the waiting list.

Bunty framed by the hoop on the 'League of Health and Beauty' float in the Guildford Carnival in 1949

We quickly settled in and got the gardens into shape. Stephen went to White House Primary School and I cycled to and from the office four times a day (home for lunch), a total of about twelve miles. We had already booked a place for Audrey at a nursing home just off the promenade at Felixstowe, not far from the *Fludyers Arms Hotel*, and as the day drew near we packed Stephen off to his Auntie Greta and Uncle Dennis at Newmarket, and Andrew off to his Auntie Marjorie and Uncle Leonard in the RAF married quarters at Felixstowe. When Audrey went into the nursing home I went to stay with friends at nearby Manor End. A day after my own 33rd birthday our daughter Elizabeth was born on 24th September 1949. A couple of weeks later we were all together again – five of us now – in Donegal Road.

By early 1950 Andrew had joined Stephen at the local school. They had made many friends in the immediate area and it was fortunate that a children's playing field had been established right behind our house. The experimental heating system kept us nicely warm in winter, and we had all the hot water we needed, but we did have some problems – on two occasions a skirting-board radiator split with a sound like gunshot and water poured out all over the carpet. All was put right by *Cranes* without any cost to us, but we did have to put up with the mess.

During our years in Donegal Road we had visitors to stay from time to time, one of whom was my Uncle Willie, and it was during his visit that on the Prom at Felixstowe a lovely child's blanket, which I had bought in Brussels before I was demobbed was lost from Elizabeth's pram. My mother and father came to see us, and so did Bunty and Arthur with Valerie and Robin.

We spent a Christmas at Bunty's travelling to London by coach and being met there by one of Arthur's reps at *Vickers*. He drove us to the works at Weybridge, where Arthur, who was quite merry after his office party, packed us all into his *Morris* car and somehow managed to drive us without mishap to Onslow Village, calling in at a farm on the way to pick up a huge turkey for our Christmas dinner. At 26 Elmside the boys, with Robin, slept in a large caravan which Arthur and a friend, Ernest, had built and which was parked for the winter in Arthur's drive. Every summer the van was towed to Milford-on-Sea to be the Harris family holiday home. Ernest and his family eventually moved to South Africa.

Our main presents for the boys and Elizabeth were too bulky to be taken with us to Guildford, so before leaving home, and out of sight of the children, I left them displayed in the living room, to be presented as a big surprise on our return. The boys' present was a tent, which I erected in the room, and Elizabeth's a red pedal motor-car. And thereby hangs a tale. It wasn't a new car (I've usually bought second-hand!) and I think I paid 15s (75p) for it. I bought it at a terraced house near Ipswich Station and went off home resting it on the handle-bar and saddle of my bike. I had noticed that the front axle was broken, so I left the car at a cycle shop on my way to Donegal Road. Some days later I collected the repaired car, bought a tin of red enamel and spent an evening or two when the children were in bed, repainting it. I must say it looked almost as good as new when I had finished; anyway, Elizabeth was thrilled with it when I handed it over after our Christmas in Surrey, and the boys were delighted with their tent.

In January 1950, when Elizabeth was four months old, Audrey's father, who had not been well for a week or so, died in Ipswich Hospital. He was 74 – not very old by today's standards. I had already booked seats for myself and the boys for the pantomime at Ipswich *Hippodrome* and, though reluctant to do so, I decided that we would go anyway since they were too young to appreciate what had happened and would have been sorely disappointed if I had told them we couldn't go.

There was a very large congregation at the funeral service in an Ipswich church, for Mr Meadlarklan was a widely known and respected figure in the grocery business. My mother-in-law, Bernard and Anne, who was then at the Convent School, were now on their own at *Rose Villa*.

In 1951 Greta and I took the boys and her girls (then just Penny and Vicky) to London for the day to visit the big Thames-side exhibition commemorating the 100th anniversary of the Great Exhibition of 1851 when Prince Albert's famous Crystal Palace was erected in Hyde Park. I don't suppose any of the children remember that outing. The Festival of Britain, while not marking the end of the austerity endured throughout the war and beyond, was regarded as a gesture of faith in a brighter future.

Elizabeth aged 2 at Donegal Road

Stephen in front with Andrew behind him

Near Waterloo 27 acres of derelict bomb-damaged London were transformed to provide such attractions as the Dome of Discovery, a floodlit Skylon, the new and permanent Royal Festival Hall, an exhibition of sculptures and 'mobiles', pleasure gardens and a large funfair. A newspaper reported at the time that the chief complaint of the public seemed to be that a cup of coffee cost 9d (about 3½p)!

In and around Ipswich our journeys were usually made by bus, but sometimes we walked the two-and-a-half miles into the town and back. At least once I pushed Elizabeth in her pram to visit Jack and José, who were then living in a house off St Helen's Street, and that must have been a three-mile walk each way. How we longed to have a car – and, yes, we finally got one. It was a 1929 *Austin 7 Tourer*, which I bought for £22. We made a few trips in it – I remember taking Audrey's mother out once – but that particular era of car ownership was short-lived. The battery gave trouble, so Bernard, then working for the AA from Stowmarket and having access to a charger, offered to have it recharged for me if I could get the car to him. We set off in good spirits – surprisingly the little *Austin* actually started – and all went well until we began to descend Whitton Hill. There was a very loud bang, the engine shuddered and we coasted to a halt. I recognised the trouble at once – a 'big end' had gone. All that we could do was push the car off the road, leave it in the entrance to a small farm and wait for a bus to get us home. What a calamity!

Next day I contacted the garage at Needham. They collected the car, told me what the damage was – confirming my own diagnosis – and as it was out of the question for me to have it repaired (I just didn't have the money!) I sold it to them for £12. That put me £10 out of pocket, so I got hold of the previous owner, who had assured me that the car was in 'good condition' and in the event we agreed to split the difference and he gave me £5 back!

Many years later I saw the old *Austin* in the garage at Needham. It had not only been repaired and put on the road gain but totally restored. If only I had kept it…!

* * * * *

My work on the *Star* continued and every now and again a really big story would break. The biggest of all was the great

148

flood of 3rd February 1953, when hurricane-force winds combined with high tides to bring disruption to the east coast as sea defences collapsed from Lerwick, Shetland, to Kent. Over 300 lives were lost and thousands were made homeless. The death toll in Felixstowe was 39, the ages of the victims ranging from babies of a few months old to elderly people of over 80. In this tragedy, almost certainly the worst in the town's history, there was more than one instance of a complete family perishing in the deluge. The sea came over the land from the Landguard end, on the river estuary side, and a wall of water six feet high swept up Langer Road towards the town.

It was night time and many people were in their beds as the torrent tore along. I heard that one man on his bike pedalled furiously ahead of the water trying to escape; whether he survived, I cannot remember. I do know that the terraced house which we had lived in for two years was flooded to the top of the front door – when the water receded one could see the tide mark. Anyone downstairs at the time would have perished. The occupants of some of the houses in the road escaped through bedroom windows, many being rescued by boat. Not so fortunate were the people living in a block of prefabs, also in Langer Road; these bungalows were just swept away from their foundations like floating match-boxes.

Up and down the coast the sea poured in, causing a tremendous amount of damage and taking many lives. Among others to visit the devastated areas, including Felixstowe, was the Duke of Edinburgh. This was a story that made big headlines for many days and we on the *Star* gave extensive coverage in words and pictures to the appalling events of that night. Our team of reporters and photographers had the busiest time of their lives. The docks area in Ipswich did not escape. The water there rose to an unprecedented level, causing a considerable amount of flooding in the area.

Another story, of quite a different nature, also made national headlines – the Suitcase Murder. One morning, in a field beside the road at Tattingstone, a few miles from Ipswich, a passer-by noticed a large suitcase which, when opened, was found to contain the dismembered body of a young man. A murder hunt began, with Detective Chief Inspector Tom Tarling in charge. The first task was to establish the identity of the victim and this was achieved when a facial photograph was published in the *Star*, the *Anglian* and the London evening papers. It was in fact the picture that appeared in the London *Evening News* that led to the identification – the victim was a young man whose home was in the East End. Macabre as it was, the photograph had been taken after his death – obvious really, though probably few people realised it at the time.

No-one was ever charged with the murder. It was strongly suspected that it was a homosexual killing, and that, because of the expert way in which the body had been dismembered, the murderer was someone with medical knowledge.

Those of us on the paper were well acquainted with members of the CID and I remained friendly with Tom Tarling for many years. On his retirement from the police he took charge of security at what was then *Eastern Electricity*. He died in 1999.

Harry Holt and I, working close together at the subs' table on the *Star*, had become great friends, as had Harry's wife, Doreen, and Audrey, and our respective children. Harry wrote a weekly column for the *Star*, 'Newsman is Talking with You', and when he was ill with a duodenal ulcer and had to go into hospital I asked Mr Wilson if I could be a guest columnist while he was away. No luck! Mr Wilson decided that our readers could wait until Harry returned to the office – probably, I suspected at the time, because it would save money! He was like that.

Over the years our children suffered the usual crop of accidents. Plastic cups were not in general use in the early '50s and one morning Andrew got out of bed and stepped on to the glass containing his orange juice, with the result that he almost severed one of his toes. On another occasion he came off his tricycle and broke his left arm. Elizabeth fell out of her high chair in the kitchen and struck her head on the solid-fuel boiler, but the worst accident, from the point of view of disfigurement, involved Stephen. He was riding his bike outside the house on the freshly gritted road when he hit the kerb and shot over the handle-bar, his chin not only striking the road but slithering along on the sharp grit. I shall never forget the look of his chin – blackened from the grit and bruising and terribly scratched, it hung down in a swollen lump for a long time. On several such occasions I was summoned from the office to meet Audrey and a wounded child at the doctor's surgery.

* * * * *

In February 1952 King George VI died and the young Princess Elizabeth ascended the Throne. We didn't join the many thousands who flocked to London for the Coronation in June 1953 but we watched the televised ceremony and state procession at a neighbour's home just round the corner from Donegal Road. The neighbour was a former RAF pilot named Ward who went on to become one of the stalwarts at Ipswich Airport – now, sadly, no longer in existence and replaced with housing. We did, however, go to London for the Trooping the Colour which took place soon after the Coronation, taking all three of our children.

About this time we had again procured our own means of transport – to wit, a 1929 996cc *AJS* motor-cycle, complete with a double-adult sidecar, and it was this machine that we used to get us all to and from Ipswich Station. The *AJS* was a heavy machine, with running boards for the rider to put his feet on, a hand-change gear lever and, of course, just a 'kick start'. The sidecar was large enough to hold two adults, one behind the other, each having a child on his or her lap, and there was a pillion on the bike itself. So, all in all, one could transport up to six people. And we did, too!

We kept the bike on the grass verge in Donegal Road, and some of the children of the neighbourhood called it 'all junk and scrap'! It wasn't easy to start and when, after a while, I began to suffer back 'trouble', which lasted for the next thirteen years, I put it down to repeated efforts – always successful in the end – to get the wretched AJS going.

It was a joy for us to be mobile again, and on the morning of our trip to London we set off in good spirits. I might have known something would happen – and sure enough, it did. We got as far as the town end of Norwich Road, about halfway to the station, when the corroded battery carrier gave way and the battery fell to the ground and shattered. It was shattering for us, too, but we didn't give up; I collected the bits of battery and stowed them in the sidecar for later disposal, and because the electrical side of the *AJS* was 'mag-dyno' (magneto-dynamo) I was able to restart it without having a functioning battery. So we continued our journey to the station, parked the bike (free then) and caught our train.

In London we joined thousands of people in The Mall and saw the Queen, the Duke and other members of the Royal Family on the balcony of the Palace. A wonderful day for us all – Stephen was then coming up to the age of 10, Andrew was 8 and Elizabeth nearly 4. Another big treat was to come that day – a proper meal at a *Lyons Corner House* to augment the picnic we had taken with us.

Back at Ipswich Station the *AJS* was there waiting for us and after several kick-starts the engine came to life and we were on our way home. It was dark by then so we had to have the lights on. This meant keeping the revs going – the higher the revs the brighter the lights, and vice versa. Next day, though, I bought a new battery and did a repair job on its carrier.

Andrew as a pupil at Whitehouse Primary School at Ipswich

From then on we had no further trouble with the *AJS* (maximum speed about 35 mph). We took Audrey's mother out in the sidecar and I distinctly remember our very first visit to Waldringfield, when Elizabeth had whooping cough and we were told that it would help her if we were to spend an hour or so beside a river at low tide when the mud was visible. Whether the visit to the Deben did any good or not I really don't know! At that time I didn't have the faintest idea that some 30 years later Audrey and I would actually be living in Waldringfield. Another popular remedy for whooping cough was to experience the smell given off by coal gas, so we tried that, too, taking Elizabeth to Ipswich, and hanging about in the vicinity of the gas works and getting her to sniff!

We made at least two longer trips with the *AJS,* one to Feltwell in Norfolk, where Leonard was then at the RAF station, and the other to spend a holiday with Brenda, Alan and family at Reepham, again in Norfolk. Just imagine: two adults, three children and all our luggage for a holiday, packed on, and into, one motor-cycle and sidecar! I don't think the authorities would look kindly on that today.

Bernard and Sheila were married in the summer of 1953 and I used the bike to help move some of their things into the flat they rented in Ipswich. On the wedding day itself my father came to look after the children while we were at the church and reception.

We Move to the Midlands

1953-1959

It was around this time that I began to consider making a move from the Evening Star. We knew that this would almost certainly mean leaving Suffolk, but Audrey gave me her full support; she knew, as I did, that it would not only be to our advantage from a career point of view but would also improve our position financially. I answered an advertisement for a sub-editor on The Birmingham Post, the city's prestigious morning paper, went to Birmingham for an interview and got the job. I had hoped to be offered a £1000 a year (my salary on the Star was then about £600), which was good money at that time, but the most the Post came up with for a start was £750. A bit disappointing but I knew that, if I came up to scratch, it wouldn't be long before I would get a rise (and I did).

So after seven years in Ipswich I joined the general news subs' table (we actually had desks) on the Post, and I settled in very well with my colleagues there – a very much larger staff than at Ipswich.

That was the easy part; the really big problem was to find somewhere for us all to live, and it wasn't solved for more than six months. In the meantime Audrey and the children stayed on in the Donegal Road house while I was living 170 miles away in Birmingham with a married cousin of my father's, Harry Hughes and his family.

I was now working at night, leaving the house at 5.30 pm, catching a bus into the city and returning in company-chartered transport at about two o'clock in the morning. My days were spent house-hunting – to rent, of course, as we didn't have the resources to buy – and the weeks went by without the slightest result; even the possibility of exchanging the tenancy of our house in Ipswich with the tenant of a council house in Birmingham came to nothing.

It was a very difficult time for Audrey, coping on her own with the three children, but she managed extremely well. We didn't see much of each other for my visits home were infrequent. I had got to Birmingham in the first place through the kindness of a friend of Harry Holt's who, though living in Ipswich, worked for a scaffolding company in the Midlands. He had an *Austin A40* car and had picked me up on the Norwich Road and dropped me off at Harry Hughes's place. On a few occasions during the six months or so that we were apart this friend was able to fit in a trip back to Ipswich at times when I was not working.

I should, perhaps, have mentioned earlier that, with great reluctance, I had parted with the *AJS* before leaving Ipswich. I couldn't have trusted it for the long journey to the Midlands, and anyway we needed the money. Another case of 'if only I'd got it now...' for it would be worth a lot today in a preserved or restored condition.

Our financial position was improving, though, and one day Harry Hughes and I went round looking at second-hand cars. Harry hadn't got one and wanted, as I did, to become mobile. He saw a nice-looking *Rover* (pre-war, of course) and I spotted an elegant *Riley* (also pre-war). In no time at all we both became car owners.

I made just one trip to Ipswich and back in the *Riley*. For the boys, especially, it was a great thrill for us to have such a smart car and we all went for a run to Shotley in it. The only trouble was that it consumed a vast amount of oil – it used a gallon on the journey to Ipswich – which meant, I suspected, that the engine was 'clapped out'. Still, it got me back to Birmingham, though I expect I had to buy another gallon of oil!

I was getting used to night work but I cannot say that I ever liked it. Though Saturdays were always free, more often than not I had to work on Sunday evenings and into the night, so getting away at weekends was always a problem. I cannot be sure, but I think that as Christmas 1953 approached the chief sub-editor, taking pity on my being separated from my family, saw to it that I had sufficient time off to go home to Audrey and the children. I certainly have no recollection of spending Christmas with Harry Hughes and family.

* * * * *

Early in 1954 someone in the office suggested that I might get help over housing if I approached the Post's company secretary about a possible mortgage. I did so at the first opportunity and was more than delighted – I was thrilled – when this sympathetic individual quite quickly came back with the answer: if I could find a house which, including legal charges, would cost no more than £2,000, the Post would give me a mortgage for that amount, at a mere 4% interest, and repayments would be deducted from my monthly salary. Yippee! We were going to be home owners at last, after twelve years of marriage. I was then 38 and Audrey 32.

Audrey joined me in Birmingham for a few days, leaving the children in someone's care (her mother's, probably) and as I still had the *Riley* we were able to use it to go house-hunting. We had picked on the pleasant suburb of Hall Green where one house that we liked proved to have dry rot and others were just above the price limit (when the legal fees were added). In the end, however, we found a semi, complete with garage that we could have 'all in' for the £2,000 available to us. It was in Bushmore Road and had a living-room, separate dining-room, kitchen, three bedrooms (one quite small) and a bathroom/toilet, gas fires in some of the rooms and a slow-burning solid fuel fire in the living-room. No central heating, I need hardly add.

We decided to take the house and a possession date was fixed. Audrey returned to Ipswich and it fell to her to prepare everything for the move, which I arranged to be carried out by an Ipswich firm. When we had to decide how Audrey, the boys and Elizabeth were to get to Birmingham, my father stepped in to help, picking them up at the Donegal Road house and driving them to Harry Hughes's, where we all spent the night before moving to Bushmore Road the next day. That was in March 1954 and we lived there for the next four years.

Stephen and Andrew went to Pitmaston School, a short walk from home, and Elizabeth started her schooling there when she was 5 in September 1954. Later, passing his 11-plus exam, Stephen went on to Moseley Grammar School, where, I remember, in a school play he took a female role (following in father's footsteps!). When it was Andrew's turn to leave Pitmaston we cashed in an insurance policy to raise the money to send him to Greenmore College at Edgbaston. Perhaps that was where the seeds of his consuming interest in professional football were sown, for the sports master was none other than the former England goalkeeper, Gill Merrick. Andrew was at Greenmore College for a year. It was unfortunate that I missed the school prize-giving, for he received an award – I think I am right in saying that it was for Scripture.

Life for us in Hall Green soon settled into a routine. My working hours at the Post were usually 6.00 pm to 1.00 am and I would leave home about 5.30 pm to catch a bus into the city, returning at about 2.00 am in the company-chartered bus which dropped off staff near their homes in the suburbs.

About once every six weeks I was on the late shift, from 10.00 pm to 6.00 am, which entailed being the sole editorial man left in the building after 2.00 am and hence responsible for making any changes that were warranted for the early-morning edition, printed at 5.30 am. Usually that meant editing short late news items for the stop-press column (so called because at that time the press had to be stopped to attach the late news 'box'). But it could involve an actual page change if something really important blew up. That edition of the paper was, therefore, way ahead of the national dailies printed much earlier for country-wide distribution.

When I was on that all-night shift I would see the presses start the 5.30 am run then, having already gathered my things together, make a dash for the central bus-stop near New Street Station to catch a Corporation bus to Hall Green, arriving home just after 6.00 am and going straight to bed until the children came home for their lunch.

A heavy responsibility rested on Audrey. When I left at 5.30 pm she would have the children entirely on her hands, and when I wasn't home until 6.00 in the morning she would have to get them up and make sure they went off to school in good time. As the boys got older and, quite naturally, wanted to be out with their friends in the evening, there were worries for her as to what they were sometimes up to.

Fortunately there was only one occasion – as far as I remember – when something serious happened and I had to be summoned from my desk. Stephen and Andrew, with other boys, were playing the dangerous game of competing with one another in running across the main road from Hall Green to Acocks Green, and Stephen, miscalculating the speed of an approaching car, was struck on the head and taken by ambulance to Birmingham Accident Hospital. Poor Audrey, what an experience for her when a policeman knocked on the door to break the news. For me, on getting a phone call at the Post, it was a dash to the hospital, where Stephen was in Casualty. It was a long night for all of us and a very lucky escape for Stephen, who broke no bones and suffered no lasting affects. I don't think he and Andrew played that dangerous game again.

Another accident during our years at Hall Green involved Elizabeth and she, too, had an ambulance trip to hospital. It happened when she and I were on my bicycle. The machine had a child's seat fixed to the tubular bar between the saddle and the handle-bar, with footrests in the area of the front wheel. As we drew in towards the kerb on the busy main road in the shopping area, Elizabeth took it into her head to put one of her feet through the spokes of the wheel, bringing us to an abrupt stop and almost throwing us to the ground. An ambulance was called and I went in it with Elizabeth to the hospital, where it was found that, though the foot was badly cut and bruised, no bones were broken. So that was another shock for Audrey when she was told that we were both at the hospital. This time I was just very late for work instead of being called out.

We paid visits to other hospitals, too. Andrew had to have periodic eyesight tests at the Children's Hospital, fortunately during the day when I was at home, and one Sunday I had to be taken in a motorcycle sidecar by our next-door neighbour, Don Cross, to a hospital that dealt with emergency dental treatment.

Audrey and I soon made friends in the area, in many cases through the children, and about a year after we had moved in, the Holts left Ipswich and came to the Midlands, buying a house quite close to ours. Harry had taken a sub-editing job on The Birmingham Despatch, rival to The Post's Evening Mail (the two were later amalgamated with The Birmingham Post & Mail Company in control). At that time the street newsvendors in the city used the familiar cry, "Patch-a-Mail."

We made some changes in the house, knocking down a pantry cupboard wall to provide a small cupboard under the stairs with access from the hall, and removing unsightly wall cupboards in the kitchen. The latter operation exposed a very badly plastered section of wall. Probably to save money when the house was built, an extremely weak mixture of plaster had obviously been used, so that when I removed the cupboards a large quantity of sand poured out, leaving deep holes. Not having any experience of plastering (at that time, anyway), I hit on the idea of covering the entire section of wall with hardboard and painting it. The result was effective, though what subsequent owners of the property thought of it if and when they found out what I had done, I neither know nor care now!

We also built – or, at least, I did under the guidance of our handy neighbour Don – a glass roof over the kitchen door area up to the back of the garage. We dealt with damp patches on the inside walls and soon discovered that the house was prone to dreadful condensation. Sometimes the living and dining-room window sills were awash with water in the morning and we tried all kinds of things to combat it, with limited success. Of course, double-glazing would have done the trick but that wasn't in vogue then. I remember, too, that an ornamental wooden fireplace surround in the dining-room was riddled with wood-worm, which we frequently sprayed with a liquid. But despite these problems the house was our home and we were very happy there, though as time went on we began to think of looking for something better. Eventually we did find a better house, but I'll come to that later.

I have already mentioned our neighbours, Don and Olive Cross: Don was quite a handyman, and he was proud, too, of his BSA motor-cycle and sidecar. Olive had lost a leg in a bicycle accident some years earlier, so she had an artificial one – in fact, I think she had two, one being a spare. They were lovely people – typical friendly Midlanders. So were the people on the other side of us, though they were quite different. There were actually three of them: the Thompsons, husband and wife, the former working in the accounts department at the Post, and a male friend who, with the wife, ran a ballroom dancing school. Quite a curious set-up really – perhaps a kind of ménage à trois!

Among our other friendly neighbours was Hal (his surname escapes me), who worked in insurance but was also an accomplished and knowledgeable musician, acting as the Post's deputy music critic. He had an allotment nearby and when he tired of it he passed it on to me. So for a while I grew our own vegetables – though I don't think I was really cut out for that kind of kind of activity.

* * * * *

My grandfather had died at the age of 87 in 1953 a little while before I joined the Post in Birmingham. My grandmother lived on for three more years and before she died in 1956, also aged 87, she came to us at Hall Green for a short holiday. She was with us for Elizabeth's fifth birthday in September 1954 – a birthday that Elizabeth still remembers well, for according to her recollection Grandma Pyatt spoilt her little party by 'taking over' and, in effect, demanding all the attention! While on the subject of my grandmother, I should mention that Grannie Dockerill died in the '50s, aged 84.

In the early days of our life at Hall Green we had no car, so all our outings were made by bus. We asked Olive Cross if there was a heath in the area where we could go for a picnic, and she recommended Hockley Heath. So off to Hockley Heath we all went one Sunday, only to find on alighting from the bus that there was no heath there at all – just the road to Stratford-upon-Avon and side roads with houses. After a vain search we settled on having our picnic on the grass verge beside the main road.

We began to venture further afield and found a delightful hilly spot past the church just off the main street of Henley-in-Arden. We had several picnics there and it was there that, on a summer's day in 1954, Audrey broke the news to me that she was sure she was expecting another baby. Confirmation at the doctor's followed – to our great delight, I may say – and in due course, on 9th April 1955, Vivienne Louise arrived on the scene. It was Easter Saturday.

During the intervening months we made all the usual preparations (having already had some practice!) and assembled the necessary equipment, including a pram (we had disposed of Elizabeth's) and carry-cot. We had kept the large drop-side cot which we had bought from Bunty when neither Valerie nor Robin required it, and today it rests in Vivienne's loft in Waldringfield.

Audrey was to have the baby at home attended by a midwife – not an unusual practice in those days – and we arranged for Elizabeth and the boys to stay with friends when the time came. Stephen was then 11½, Andrew was 10 and Elizabeth 5½. I arranged with my chief sub to take a week's holiday starting from 'D-Day'. Everything went according to plan. Surprisingly (it may be thought) we all went to the cinema on Thursday the 7th to see The Student Prince. As the next day was Good Friday, when the Post (at that time) wasn't published, I had the night off.

Good Friday came and I got the boys and Elizabeth settled with our friends. Audrey and I went to bed that night with little expectation of getting much sleep. And we didn't. Vivienne started on the last 'lap' of her journey into the world at around 4.00 am, the midwife was summoned (I must have dashed to the Holts to use their phone as we didn't have one) and on her arrival I was quickly shooed out of the bedroom to complete my vigil sitting on the bottom of the stairs – husbands weren't then allowed to be present at births. All went well, my prayers had been answered and we had another daughter to redress the family imbalance.

For a short time I had a local authority home-help to assist me in the house. She wasn't very good at her job – at least, not as a cook – and one day we had to 'suffer' her pièce de résistance, a bread pudding. Not a bread-and-butter pudding – just a bread one. It was so awful that we had to throw it away. I was glad when she finished her time with us and I was in charge again; even more glad when Audrey was well enough to take over and I was back at my desk at the Post.

Being at home during the day enabled me to give Audrey a helping hand and the time came when, on my own, I was able to take Vivienne out in her pram, though sometimes we would go together. It may seem strange but our favourite walk was through the gardens of a local cemetery.

At Christmas time a treat for the children was to be taken into Birmingham to the city's biggest store, Lewis's, where on the top floor, several storeys up, Father Christmas had his grotto. We used to join a queue on the ground floor and move very slowly, storey by storey, to the top, where, having had the dubious experience of sitting on Father Christmas's knee, the boys and Elizabeth groped in a big box for their presents. Happy days!

When Vivienne reached the toddling stage she discovered a small gap in the hedge between our garden and the Thompsons', and took great delight in going through it to be fussed over by Mrs Thompson in her kitchen. I remember she heated the room by lighting the gas oven and leaving the door open, though I'm sure she closed the door when Vivienne was there.

At intervals over the next few years I made various attempts to move from night to day work without success until 1959 (and I'll come to that later). Although the editor-in-chief of the *Post & Mail* group, Frank Owen, was my former colleague at Wisbech, he wouldn't help me – rightly, I'm sure – by making an exception to the house rule that precluded switching from the morning to the evening paper, at least as far as sub-editors were concerned. So there was no joy for me there. In the course of other attempts to make a move to day work I went to London for interviews (*BBC* and *Pye*, the radio and television manufacturers), Wales (*British Nylon Spinners*) and Carlisle (evening paper).

In June 1956 we borrowed my second cousin Harry's *Hillman Minx* (he had sold the *Rover*) to drive to Ipswich for Anne's wedding. She and Henry Petch were married at St Augustine's Church and among the guests was the Rev Frank Tucker-Harvey, an old friend of the Meadlarklan family, who had married us at Stowmarket in 1942. The next day he baptized Vivienne at his own church in Ipswich.

The house in Bushmore Road

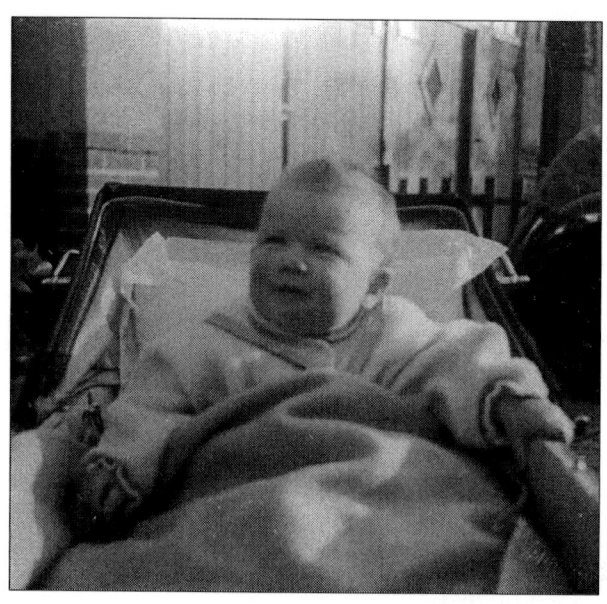

Vivienne in 1955

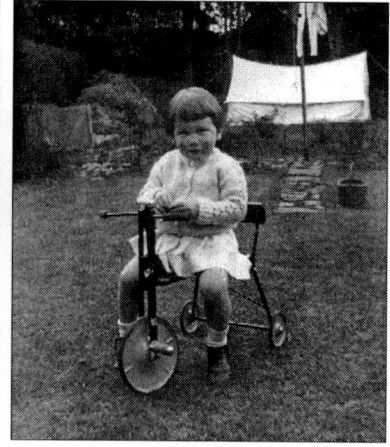

Vivienne aged 2 on the beach at Felixstowe... and at Bushmore Road with hints of future camping trips in the background!

With Stephen at Moseley Grammar School and Andrew at Greenmore College, Elizabeth was the only one of the children continuing at Pitmaston School, where the headmaster was a Harry Walker. That name may not mean anything to most people today but he was a well-known personality in broadcasting in the '50s and '60s whose speciality was swimming commentaries. When any national swimming events were held we always tuned in to listen to him on the radio.

I had a very good child's swing made for Elizabeth. Our neighbour Olive's father was a blacksmith and he constructed a really substantial swing, far superior to those on offer in the shops at the time. It must have been in 1956 when we had the swing and we took it with us to Sutton Coldfield, Leamington Spa and Needham Market before finally parting with it to a journalist colleague who had a young daughter – to the disgust of Elizabeth and Vivienne, who thought we should have kept it.

It was in 1956 that we acquired our first television set – black and white, of course. We began by renting it, then after about a year we ended the rental agreement and bought it. One of the first programmes we viewed was the Cup Final, in the company of a *Post* sub-editor colleague, his wife and small son. I remember that we pulled the curtains across and sat in complete darkness except for the illuminated screen.

When my colleague later invited us to tea in return, Audrey met with a nasty mishap on our way home. She stumbled as she was getting on the bus, gashing her leg badly on the boarding step. The wound took a long time to heal.

At intervals we had several visitors. My parents came to stay, as did Bunty and Arthur with Valerie and Robin; Anne and Henry; and Brenda and her first husband, Alan. Then there was a Christmas when we were due to stay with Harry Hughes and

Dorothy, now living in the Birmingham suburb of Great Barr. Dorothy made all the usual preparations for a family gathering, whereas we felt there was no need for us to stock up – which was unfortunate because just before Christmas the boys went down with chickenpox and we had to stay at home. Poor Dorothy with all the food she had got, and poor us with just some hastily-purchased pork for our Christmas dinner!

An even more memorable occasion was when, to borrow a commercial phrase, we 'double booked' for Christmas. We had invited my father and mother, and somehow or other we had also sent an invitation to Marjorie, Leonard and their children, Michael and Mary, and we only had a two-and-a-half bedroom house! But there was no question of putting anyone off – we just had to think of a way we would be able to cope with eleven people. The upshot was that Stephen, Andrew and Michael were found beds with the Holts and the rest of us made do. We were all together for meals, of course.

A lasting memory of that Christmas, especially for our children, is of the presents-opening 'ceremony', carried out with almost military precision in the Cuming fashion. If we had had *our* way, presents would have been opened straight after breakfast, and we blamed ourselves for not insisting on this, as we had every right to do as hosts. But no, we gave in to Marjorie and Leonard (really it was to Leonard) and the ritual was delayed until mid-afternoon following Christmas dinner. What an ordeal it must have been for the children. The ritual itself took the form of Leonard holding a piece of paper and pencil, and writing down the details of each present and the name of the giver as, one at a time, each child opened a gift. All very efficient, of course, but not exactly *our* way of doing things.

On our trips into Birmingham we invariably wandered round the shops and stalls in the famous Bull Ring, and one year I bought the children's Christmas presents there.

The boys were in the Scout movement, perhaps Andrew was then a Cub. At any rate, his usual practice on the way home each week was to call in at a fish and chip shop and buy a pickled onion for a penny. I know he still remembers that.

We had more than one 'holiday at home' in the summer, going on trips by bus, but one year Bunty and Arthur offered to let us have their house in Guildford while they were at their caravan at Milford-on-Sea. Vivienne was just a baby then and needed the pram, so we took advantage of the railway's luggage-in-advance facility, packed the pram with some of our luggage, and I pushed it a mile or so to Hall Green Station for onward conveyance to Guildford, where I had to collect it the day after our arrival. On the day of our departure we actually took a taxi to New Street Station. On the train I was not very careful when putting a suitcase on the rack above the seat where Audrey was sitting with Vivienne in her arms. The case slipped from my grasp and fell, giving poor little Vivienne a glancing blow on her head – not a good start to our holiday, but I was thankful that Vivienne suffered little hurt. It could certainly have been much worse.

* * * * *

By 1957 we had accumulated enough money to consider looking again for a car of our own. On my way to work by bus I had seen several used car displays, so it wasn't difficult to pick on a suitable one for further investigation. This I did when my eye caught sight of a black 1939 *Hillman Minx* which looked to be in good condition even if it was 18 years old. I bought it for £125 – quite a lot of money to me then – and it served us well for nearly three years. We drove to Ipswich and back in it at least twice. The first occasion was when we stayed with Audrey's mother in Foxhall Road for a summer holiday, using the car for daily trips to the coast.

The car was pretty basic compared with those of today. It didn't even have hydraulic brakes – they were operated by cables. Its top speed was about 50mph (downhill) and its cruising speed 35-40mph. Our second journey to Ipswich, for a Christmas with Anne and Henry, was made in the foggiest weather I have ever encountered. With the windscreen open (a facility not now available, as far as I know) I could just about see the nearside kerb, so it's easy to understand that the journey of about 165 miles took us all day, from breakfast to early evening. But we made it without mishap.

Having the car opened up a new world to us in the Midlands. We began to explore more distant parts: the Lickey Hills, not far from the then giant *Austin-Morris* works at Longbridge on the other side of Birmingham, the Malvern Hills, the Burton Dasset Hills and Stratford-upon-Avon – though we had already had several picnics on the banks of the Avon at Stratford, opposite the Shakespeare Memorial Theatre, by using buses. The one snag when we made these outings on a Sunday was that I was invariably due to start work at 6.00 pm, so we had to leave for home earlier than we would have wished. Many a cricket session with the boys on the Lickey Hills had to be brought to a hasty conclusion when I noticed the time.

Another spot which Stephen, especially, found to his liking was Earlswood Lakes. There, Stephen spent many a happy hour fishing. Once, standing beside him on a small wooden jetty, I dropped my keys, which went through the slats and disappeared in the muddy water. We did manage to retrieve them – I think by fishing around with the rod and line, though I can't be sure.

We had another member of the Meadlarklan family to visit, too. Audrey's brother Bernard had lived with us in Bushmore Road for a few months while job hunting. He eventually took a job as manager of a grocery store at Yardley, another outer Birmingham suburb, and he and Sheila lived in a flat over the shop, so we were able to exchange visits. It must have been the winter of 1957-58, for as I was not at that time able to indulge in the 'luxury' of anti-freeze in the *Hillman*'s cooling system, I had a small oil lamp which I used to put under the sump to provide just enough heat to keep the engine warm. I even took this lamp with me to Bernard's and put it in position when we parked behind his shop. (Talk about Heath Robinson, if that means anything to my readers!)

By this time – late 1957 – we began to think about making a move. We settled on an area of Four Oaks, an attractive part of Sutton Coldfield, where a new housing estate was springing up, and our final choice was a semi-detached house in Leyhill Road which was well under construction.

We had little difficulty in selling the house in Bushmore Road despite its drawbacks! I made a small profit and settled my mortgage account with *The Birmingham Post,* as I had agreed to do if I sold the house, having no further mortgage with the company. Apart from the attractions of the Four Oaks house itself there was another inducement – the developer would pay all the legal charges provided I took out a mortgage with the *Woolwich Building Society.* And this I did, of course. I think the house cost £2,750; today it's probably worth more than £200,000!

A matter which had to be investigated before we left Hall Green was transportation from Sutton Coldfield to Birmingham. There were buses and trains – even a station at Four Oaks – but nothing operated late into the night. Although there was nowhere to park a car at or near the office, I realised I would need some kind of transport for the ten miles into the centre of Birmingham and back again in the early hours. So I bought a second-hand moped, a French *Mobylette,* for £23, using this machine daily (or, rather, nightly) for nearly two years.

We paid one or two visits to Four Oaks to see how things were getting on, and eventually an occupation date was fixed, tying in with the agreed date when we would leave Bushmore Road.

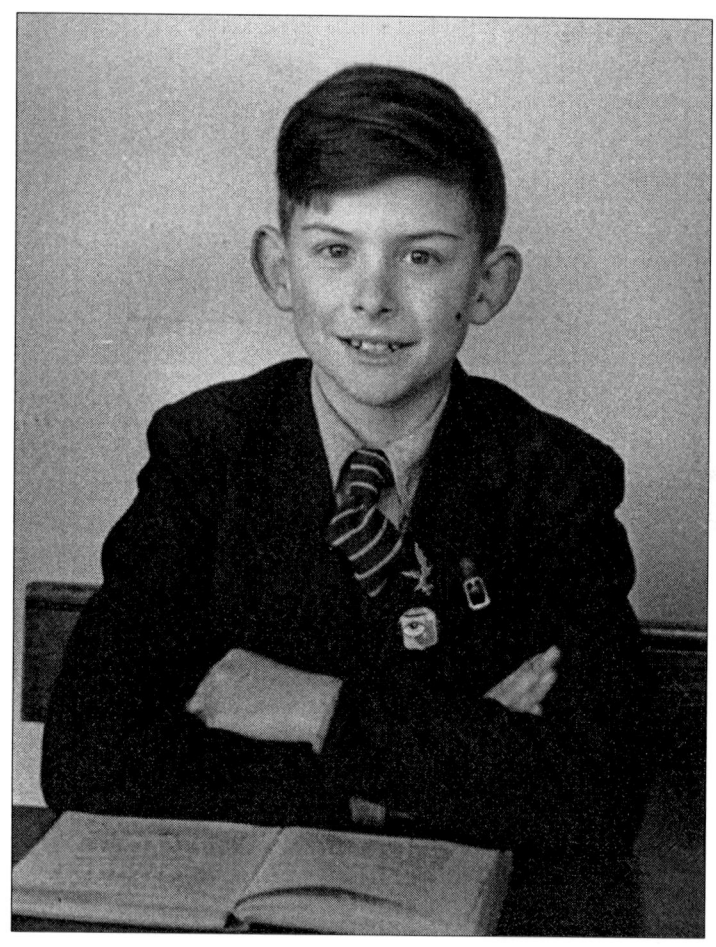

Stephen when a pupil at Moseley Grammar School

I made arrangements with a removals firm and we were all set to go when – to my horror – the builders told me the house would not be ready for another week! I think this was the one and only time in my life when I really lost my temper – to such an extent that I banged my fist on the development manager's desk and demanded to know where he thought my family would live in the meantime: "...in the open air of Sutton Park?" I asked. Rather to my surprise my outburst – for that is what it was – proved effective, and the manager, having calmed me down, said that, providing we accepted the house as it stood, with emulsioned walls still drying out and the kitchen floor not yet tiled, we could move in on the agreed date. And so we did, having to make sure for the first week or more that all items of furniture were kept well away from the walls, and evacuating the kitchen while the floor was being laid.

We soon settled in: Stephen transferred to Bishop Vesey's Grammar School, Andrew to Ryland-Bedford Secondary Modern and Elizabeth to Mere Green Primary School. Again we found that we had friendly neighbours: Charles and Anne Stuart, the Farrows, whose daughter, Christine, was about the same age as Elizabeth, and the Wychbolds, next door, among others in the road. Our first task was to turn the front and back areas of the property into presentable gardens; we grassed the front, spent many hours removing large stones at the back – at the end of which was a wood – finally laying grass there, too, and made a terrace across the back of the house.

I was exposed to the elements when I rode the moped to and from Birmingham. This was all right in the summer but certainly not in the winter when I often used to arrive at the office feeling so cold that it took me a quarter of an hour to thaw out. The moped had no windshield or leg guards, and my clothing was not exactly suited to motor-cycling. I had no helmet either!

By this time I had moved from news sub-editing to work on special features under a most meticulous man, Sydney Dodd, who had previously been night editor. The *Post*'s standards were extremely high, for which I was very grateful when in later years I myself took on the responsibilities of an editor. In all the editorial departments great stress was set on achieving accuracy in everything that was going to appear in the paper, and in content regard was always paid to good taste. There were many house rules covering spelling and style. My hours were still 6.00 pm to 1.00 am and I rode home through the deserted streets of the city in the early hours. Once or twice the *Mobylette*'s chain broke and I had to walk a mile or so pushing the machine if I couldn't fix it by the roadside. Fortunately this only happened on my homeward journeys.

Sutton Coldfield lying to the north of Birmingham, we started to visit such places as Tamworth and Lichfield in adjoining Staffordshire. We also took the children to the zoo at Dudley. Contrary to what a lot of people who haven't been there think, the Midlands have much to offer. Of course, there are extensive industrial areas – and especially today, much traffic congestion – but there is a great deal of very pleasant countryside and there are many interesting places and attractions to visit.

One trip we made was to Burbage near Hinckley in Leicestershire, where my war-time comrade, 'Judge' Henson, back in practice as a solicitor, was living with his large family. Having several children, he needed a big car, but we were rather taken back when the vehicle turned out to be a *Rolls-Royce*! An oldish one, maybe, but it occurred to me that even so he must be doing very well with his legal work. The house was appropriately large and up-market, too!

* * * * *

A memorable journey was undertaken by Stephen on his own. He was about 15 at the time and decided that he would cycle to Ipswich and back, staying with his grandmother for a week – a round trip on his bike of some 340 miles. I suppose Audrey and I had some misgivings about the venture but we agreed to it on condition that he spent a few weeks in training. And this he did, going out in the summer evenings for rides of 20 or 30 miles.

The route would be via Nuneaton, Market Harborough, Kettering, Huntingdon, Cambridge, Newmarket, Bury St Edmunds, Stowmarket and Needham, and the journey was to take two days. We looked at the map to see where the halfway stage would be and found out that there was a youth hostel near Huntingdon, so we booked him in there for the night.

The day of departure came. Travelling light, with just enough food and drink to see him through the day, Stephen set off on his bike, which had three speeds rather than the multitude of gears fitted today. I'm sure that Audrey and I spent several anxious hours before we made a phone call to the hostel in the evening, but we needn't have worried for Stephen had arrived safe and sound after his 85-mile ride and was ready for bed to get in a good night's sleep before setting off again next day.

He successfully accomplished the second leg of his ride, put his bike in his grandmother's shed as soon as he arrived and didn't look at it again until the time came for him to cycle home a week later. The return journey was made in the same way, with a night spent at the youth hostel. All in all a most successful trip and we were very proud of our enterprising son. It was his own idea and he did everything on his own. Well done!

We got on very well with our neighbours, the Farrows, across the road – Mr Farrow had a Government job in Birmingham and I remember that he had one of the earliest *Ford Cortina*s. His very pleasant wife had a most peculiar habit – she kept all her money in shoe boxes in a wardrobe! I know that because she showed me – very trusting! The Farrows' young daughter, Christine, was Elizabeth's friend, and on Sundays I used to take them to church at Four Oaks.

Mr Wychbold, next door to us, was a schoolmaster and with exams approaching he gave extra maths lessons to Stephen. Anne and Charles Stuart, who had two very young children, lived a bit further down the road. They were both very academic. Charles had a top job with *British Rail*, as it was then. Later, after leaving the Midlands, he moved to an even bigger job with *British Airways* and on his retirement in his late fifties he set up his own airline operating from Exeter Airport. Sadly, he died at the age of 64. Audrey and I kept in touch with the Stuarts over the intervening years and I continue to do so with Anne. Elizabeth, I know, remembers Anne Stuart giving her English lessons, in particular explaining what prefixes and suffixes are all about.

Another friend living nearby was Joyce Crowe (I've forgotten her husband's name). Audrey and I used to babysit for her. She was a great fan of Frank Sinatra, who was then in his heyday, and had lots of his records.

A Taste of the Motor Industry

1959-1964

One day I spotted an advertisement in *The Post* that interested me. It was for a journalist to edit the *Standard Triumph News*, an in-house monthly newspaper for employees of the motor manufacturing group at Coventry. A day job in sight at last – or at least the possibility of one! I applied by post, was given an interview date and went to Coventry by train. At the outset I was almost put off by the (typically industrial) procedure which preceded the interview. I had to check in at a building at the main factory entrance, rather like a labour exchange, state my business and wait while inquiries were made.

In the event I was escorted to an office where a charming man – he turned out to be the father-in-law of the company's chief executive, Alec Dick – interviewed me. He explained that the editor of the *Standard Triumph News* was to take over as editor of the *Standard Triumph Review*, a monthly magazine for *Standard* and *Triumph* owners, which he himself had been running, so a replacement was needed for the newspaper.

I was offered the job, accepted it and after a month left *The Post* in Birmingham for *Standard Triumph* in Coventry – my first, and only, taste of industrial life, even if my role was that of a journalist. I took over from a younger man, Fred Bryant, and edited the paper – writing most of what went in it – for the next three years, from 1959 to 1962.

Alec Dick was a motor industry prodigy. He had joined the *Standard Motor Company* as an apprentice, in the days when the renowned Captain Black ran the company, and rose to the very top to become the chief executive of *Standard Triumph* at the time when the *Standard Vanguard* led the way in post-war design and the famous *TRs* were collecting rally awards. I arrived on the scene just as the *Triumph Herald* was about to be launched with what I consider to be one of the best ever advertising slogans for cars, 'A new experience in motoring'. It certainly was, for the *Herald*, one of the few remaining cars to be built on a chassis, offered several novel features: not only disc brakes but rack-and-pinion steering and independent suspension all round, almost unheard of at the time.

As editor of the company's newspaper I had access to all departments of the company and all the workshops where manufacturing and assembly took place. All the time I was searching for news and there was plenty to be had on the huge factory site. I had contacts in each department who provided me with items for the paper, which was printed in Coventry and sent by post to the homes of every one of the several thousand employees, rather than distributed within the factory itself.

My immediate boss was a man named McDonagh, the company's industrial relations executive, whose job, in effect, was to keep the peace between management and labour and to ensure the smooth running of production. Although I wrote most of what appeared in print, with the assistance of a secretary, Anne Badnadge, who was responsible for women's features, McDonagh would from time to time write a piece which had to be included. This was usually when the management wanted a particular message putting across, and, coming as I did from the independent world of newspapers where an objective view was taken, I wasn't always too happy about this. Nevertheless, I enjoyed my days at *Standard Triumph*, wandering around the factory, seeing for myself just how cars were mass produced, collecting material for news reports, arranging for pictures (we had our own picture and film-making unit) and editing and designing the paper. Everyone was helpful and I got to know many people. The printers, too, were a friendly and co-operative crowd, and it was good to keep my hand in at their works when the paper had to be 'made up' and printed – or 'put to bed', as we say in the newspaper world.

Sadly, I wasn't given a company car! But when McDonagh saw my ancient *Hillman Minx*, which I was using to drive from Sutton Coldfield and back each day, he took pity on me and arranged that I should buy, at a very low price, a company *Triumph Mayflower* that was being used by the supply director's wife. This was a '50s car in excellent condition and I later found that it was, in fact, the very last of the 30,000-odd *Mayflower*s to come off the production line.

The *Mayflower* was almost a mini *Rolls Royce* – to us, anyway. Great was the excitement when I arrived home in it for the first time. Right away, we all piled in and I drove the car into Sutton Park, about a mile and half away. But excitement turned to dismay when it came to a halt and would not restart. Believe it or not we had run out of petrol! I had assumed (something one should never do!) that the tank had been filled before I left the factory, so I had either failed to look at the gauge or it wasn't registering properly. Anyway, there we were stuck in Sutton Park, and I just cannot remember how we got the petrol we needed. I must have prevailed on another motorist to give me a lift to the nearest garage, borrowed a can and, probably, returned on foot to the *Mayflower* and my waiting family – not a promising start! The *Mayflower* served us well for the next three years, and was, in fact, the first of my long line of modern cars.

* * * * *

New features at the Coventry factory complex which were introduced soon after my arrival were a computer building and a more modern telephone system and exchange, also in its own building, to be followed later on by the construction of a much larger assembly building where the running tracks, on which the cars were put together, were under continuous surveillance by means of strategically placed closed-circuit television cameras. Very novel at that time, I can say.

Computers were barely out of their infancy at the time and few industries had started to use them. They were really big, hence the need for a special building to house them. The new telephone exchange was equipped with a cordless switchboard, another innovation.

My search for news took me not only to all parts of the factory site but to the competitions department at Allesley, a couple of miles away, to the *Massey-Ferguson* tractor plant, which was then part of the *Standard Triumph* group, and to another motor factory which had at one time been the *Daimler* works.

The competitions manager at the time was Ken Richardson and among the rally drivers I met was Paddy Hopkirk. With *TR*s then in great demand and performing well in competitions, it may be remembered that in a 1960s Le Mans three of them finished in sequence well up in front of the field and leading their class. I believe that two of these cars still exist.

The company also ran a scheme whereby American sports car enthusiasts wishing to take new *TR*s back to the States were able to pay for a package deal giving them an Atlantic crossing in a luxury liner, the chance to see the production line, a new car and a guided European tour before embarking for home.

They weren't the only visitors to the factory. There was a department to provide guided tours and occasionally a celebrity would pay us a visit. One was the late Kenneth More, the film star, and I remember having tea with him after he had been shown round. There was the occasion, too, when a concert was given for employees, the star of the show being the late Dusty Springfield. I also recall an occasion when I had coffee with a radio comedian who always took his large dog round with him. I think it must have been during a *Workers' Playtime* at the *Massey-Ferguson* works.

It was at about this time that Britain's first really long stretch of motorway, the M1, was opened. The motorway lies only a few miles from Coventry and a linking part of the then A45 was renamed the M45. As there was then no speed limit on motorways we were soon hearing of the company's executives and testers joining in a mad rush to London at 100 mph and more. It wasn't long before the 70 mph limit was imposed, but that didn't deter some drivers. I can recall being driven to Sutton Coldfield by one of the company's managers in a hotted-up *Standard Vanguard* estate and noticing that the speedometer needle touched the 120 mph mark on a stretch of ordinary dual-carriageway – very naughty! And that was about 40 years ago!

It was while we were living in Leyhill Road that Andrew, then a pupil at Riland Bedford School, was injured during a school rugby match. In the course of making a tackle he fell awkwardly, breaking his left arm. Initially, he was taken to the hospital in Sutton Coldfield and there the fracture was found to be so severe that he was transferred to Birmingham Accident Hospital for it to be set under anaesthetic; for that, parental permission was required, so I was summoned from the factory at Coventry to be at Andrew's bedside and consent to the operation. Yet another Pyatt emergency! I had become used to them by now, and this one, like the others, soon became just a memory.

Although we were very happy at Sutton Coldfield, liking the area and the house we were in, we began to think of moving nearer to Coventry. Kenilworth attracted us and we saw that some suitable houses were being built near to the town centre.

Unfortunately for us they were all spoken for, but we discovered that the builders were erecting similar houses at New Cubbington, on the outskirts of Leamington Spa, which is a quite delightful town and only about seven miles from Coventry.

This was in the summer of 1960. Stephen would be 17 in September and ready to leave school. He wanted to become a motor engineer and as *Standard Triumph* had an apprentice scheme he applied to the company and secured a place. This involved attendance at Coventry Technical College to earn a City and Guilds diploma, and the fact that he would be starting there in the late summer was another reason for us to be nearer Coventry.

We chose one of the houses being built at New Cubbington – just in time, as it turned out, to specify some changes from the standard design. The main change was to reduce slightly the size of one of the three bedrooms and to have the toilet and bathroom as one, so as to provide the fourth bedroom we needed. Downstairs we had the outside lavatory incorporated with a cupboard area in the hall to provide another indoor toilet. I still find it incredible that these alterations added a mere £12 to the cost of the house!

* * * * *

Again there was a hitch, though one about which we were given good notice: the house would not be ready until three months later than the original possession date. However, this time the builders were quite helpful: they had a very old property, then vacant, in the village of Barford, about four or five miles on the other side of Leamington, which they could let us have at a nominal rent until the house in Dunblane Drive, New Cubbington, was ready. We accepted this offer as we really had no option, even though the Barford house was in a poor state of repair. I remember that our friend Mrs Farrow helped Audrey

182

and me carry out a big cleaning operation before we moved in, having again had no difficulty in selling our house in Sutton Coldfield. Outside the back door there was an attached barn-like area with house martins' nests in its beamed roof.

It was from the house in Barford that we set out that August for the last holiday we were to have as a complete family. We went to the small Devonshire resort of Mortehoe to camp under canvas with Anne, Henry and baby Christopher. It was a holiday to be remembered, for we had to survive heavy rain for several days at the start, and Vivienne, then aged 5, got lost on the enormous beach at Woolacombe.

Elizabeth
in 1960

Andrew aged 15

I think Anne and Henry had some sort of frame tent, but as we didn't have one at all we had to drive via Bristol to pick up a hired tent, which turned out to be a heavy duty Army-style bell tent with a very thick central pole. Just how we managed to get it into the *Mayflower* as well as ourselves and our luggage, I shall never know – but we did and I think we even erected it at an overnight stop where we linked up with Anne and Henry *en route* to Devon. They were with us for the return journey and I recall that on arrival at Barford Anne cooked steaks which we had bought on the way home, and they stayed the night before heading back to Suffolk.

But to the holiday itself. Despite the rain we were comfortable in our tent – until one night there was such a deluge that the boys and I, with Henry's help, had to get up and dig a channel round the outside so the accumulated water could flow away – perhaps to someone else's tent! Even so a few things got wet, and it wasn't pleasant doing the cooking in the open on a camp stove between the two tents. In fact, the weather was so bad that Henry – with, I must confess, a little support from Audrey – suggested that we should abandon camp and either go somewhere else or make for home. "No way," declared Anne and yours truly! And our view, supported, I'm sure, by the children, prevailed. We stayed on and the sun shone, on and off, for the remainder of the holiday, enabling us to swim, play tennis on the beach and explore the rocks.

The day when Vivienne got lost – at least to us for a while – is one that I shall never forget. As I have said, we were on the vast expanse of beach at Woolacombe, along with many hundreds of others in family groups, when we noticed that Vivienne wasn't with us, and a quick look round produced no sign of her. Fearing that she had wandered into the sea, I raced to the water and, still in my long trousers, strode in and began a frantic search. In the meantime someone had alerted the crew of a patrolling *Land Rover* and they put out an alert through a megaphone. Very soon, though it seemed like ages, these was a response: Vivienne was not many yards away from where we had been sitting and had attached herself to another family, completely unaware of the panic into which we had all been thrown. I was recalled from the sea, and never have I been so thankful as I was when I found my little daughter safely reunited with Audrey, Elizabeth and the boys.

Other memories of that holiday: Henry and I driving down to the village bakery every morning to buy freshly-baked bread rolls, and the day we went to Ilfracombe, got soaking wet and went to a café for a meal where we were provided with a back room to ourselves!

Back in Barford, Stephen started his apprenticeship at *Standard Triumph* within a few days, and as he had to be at work an hour earlier than I did he moved in with his cousin, Michael Cuming, who had a room in Coventry while he was studying at the Lanchester College of Technology. Stephen stayed on with Michael until we eventually moved into the house in New Cubbington.

Elizabeth and Andrew started at new schools in Leamington. Andrew went to Blackdown High School and Elizabeth to a primary school near to where we were going to live when the house was ready. I took them into Leamington each morning and they made their own way back to Barford by bus. For Vivienne the school in the village was her first – and the one she enjoyed going to more than any other, she tells me.

Our days at Barford passed happily, but we were very pleased when the time came for us to move into our new house. Yet again we were fortunate to have very friendly next-door neighbours, Christine and Stan Sabin, who, I believe, are still in their Dunblane Road house to this day.

Elizabeth and Andrew were already settled in their new schools and Vivienne joined Elizabeth at the primary. Stephen travelled to Coventry by bus, either returning by the same means or being given a lift; sometimes he came home with me. Later on Stan Sabin gave him his old motor-cycle, which he used to go to work and back. One day, taking a bend too fast, he veered off the road across a verge and into and along a ditch – fortunately without serious injury, though he collected a lot of scratches.

The *Mayflower* was in frequent demand. With Stephen driving, he and Andrew would borrow it to go out with their friends. On one occasion something happened that I knew nothing about until several years later. Apparently Stephen 'pushed' the car just a bit too hard and for too long with the result that the engine seized up. After waiting a while for it to cool down they got the *Mayflower* going again and drove home.

Not long after this, and in complete ignorance of the incident, I drove the car to Scotland with Audrey and the girls for a holiday with friends, Olive and Roy Beatt, and on the return journey we became aware of a mysterious tinkling sound coming from the engine. We got home all right and I told Stephen what we had heard. In no time he had the cylinder head off to find that some of the piston rings had broken and the bits had been flying around in the cylinders. He was able to fit new rings and said no more about it, though he obviously knew what had caused the problem, and he didn't get around to telling me until many years later! I just think we were very fortunate to have made the trip and got back home before the engine packed up completely!

Another time when the boys borrowed the *Mayflower* for an evening out, they parked the car just off the hard surface of the crowded car park at a local hostelry, *Chesford Grange,* only to find, when the time came to return home, that it had sunk almost to the hub caps in the soft ground. They had to leave the *Mayflower* there for the night and when I went with them the next morning, a Saturday, we had to find someone with a tractor to tow the car on to the hard surface, where we hosed it down.

In due course Stephen acquired his own cars, the first two being *Morris*es of 1930s' vintage. One night he ran out of petrol about a dozen miles from home on the road to Banbury, left the car on the forecourt of a closed garage, thumbed a lift into Leamington and woke me up. It was after midnight but luckily there was an all-night filling station in the town and we were able to get some petrol in a can. Then we drove in the *Mayflower* to his 'abandoned' car and replenished the tank for the drive back.

There was an incident with his second car, too, this time a bit nearer home. Taking a country road bend a bit too fast, Stephen drove his car over the verge and through a closed gate into a field. He was able to drive home but next morning, again on a Saturday, Andrew and I had to help him repair the farmer's hedge and gate.

Over the later years at Hall Green, then at Sutton Coldfield and now at Leamington Spa, both Stephen and Andrew had a variety of part-time jobs – paper rounds, delivering groceries and meat, cleaning cars and so on. Andrew worked at a local filling station for a time, then at a nearby pub and in the kitchen of a restaurant in the town. He also delivered flowers, taking the part-time job mainly because, having the use of a van, he was able to practise his driving – he had passed his test on Christmas Eve of all times! I think Stephen also helped a local builder.

It was during our time in Leamington that Audrey had to go into hospital twice for operations on varicose veins. On the second occasion she also had surgery on her thyroid gland. Somehow we managed at home, with help from our kind neighbour, Christine. During Audrey's second stay in hospital we had visitors. Audrey's sister, Greta, with Dennis and their children, who had emigrated to Canada in 1957, were back in England for about six months, but had decided to return to the Toronto area. We hadn't seen them during their stay and it was just unfortunate that they left it to the last minute to come to visit us. In the circumstances they stayed at a hotel in

Leamington, though they spent a couple of days with the children and me and were able to visit Audrey in hospital.

* * * * *

In 1962 my old boss at *The Birmingham Post* got in touch to offer me a more senior job in his department than I had had before, at a higher salary. My hours would be more amenable too – 2.00 pm to 10.00 pm (which invariably turned out to be 11.00 pm). So after three years at *Standard Triumph* I returned to *The Post*. I was able to travel by train to Snow Hill Station in the city, leaving my car, for free, in a small car park not too far from Leamington Station.

My work at *The Post* now embraced handling a wide range of special features, the most important of which, and one of which we were particularly proud, being a comprehensive broadsheet pull-out of several pages at the time of the consecration of the new Coventry Cathedral. The old Cathedral had been very severely damaged by German bombing, but now the ruins had been tidied up and the new building was designed to merge with the remains of the old. It is a magnificent edifice, in the modern style, and several famous artists contributed to its adornment, each of them providing a specially written article for our commemorative supplement. It was my job to edit their copy and share in the design and presentation.

In the winter of 1963 there was a big freeze-up throughout the country. My steam trains to Birmingham, covered in frozen snow, managed to keep going though I was sometimes late for work. On returning to my car in the early hours it used to take many minutes to clear the frozen windscreen and get the engine started. Most people in our area of the town reported frozen pipes and I remember that for several days our water came from delivery trucks.

The saddest time of our ten years or so in the Midlands was one weekend when four of the boys' friends were killed, and two others seriously injured, in a car crash. It happened late one evening: Stephen was out somewhere else with Dot, then his girl-friend, and Andrew was with a party of six young people. They had gone out in a small van driven by Roger Parry, a particular friend of both Stephen and Andrew, and some other friends were in another car.

When the time came to make for home the six, including one young girl, packed themselves into Roger's van but there was no room left for Andrew, so he came home – safely – in the car, knowing nothing about the fatal crash until later in the night. Taking a bend in the road near the Warwickshire village of Preston Bagot, Roger apparently lost control of the van which mounted a verge and crashed into a tree. One of the four killed was the young girl.

Audrey and I were in bed when Andrew came home, and he was soon fast asleep. It was only later when a policeman came to the house to check on Andrew that we heard the dreadful news. Shocked and upset as we were, we also felt so very thankful that, by a miraculous chance, Andrew had not been one of the victims.

Another tragedy which marked our years at Leamington was the sudden death of Dot's elder brother, Bob. He was only 22, and an all-round sportsman who appeared to be extremely fit, but he collapsed in the ring after boxing at a local club and was pronounced dead on the spot. It was a great shock for his family and friends. The inquest evidence was that he had died of viral pneumonia.

With the end of his schooldays approaching, Andrew had to decide on his future career. One option which he briefly considered was to join the Army, perhaps as a paratrooper, and I recall that a recruiting sergeant came to the house one day to discuss the matter. He also spent a few months as a reporter on the *Leamington Spa Courier,* but that didn't work out and he took a job in the Inland Revenue office in Coventry before moving on to the spares department at *Standard Triumph.* So for a while there were three of us working for the motor company.

Elizabeth, having passed the 11-plus exam, was now a pupil at Kenilworth Grammar School.

By this time I had sold the *Triumph Mayflower* and bought a *Standard Ensign.* As a former taxi it had covered many miles! We had one holiday using the *Ensign* at the Norfolk resort of Hemsby with Anne and Henry and their two boys. I remember it well because, while Anne and Henry had a comparatively short distance to drive to Hemsby it was a long journey for us from the Midlands, the roads were congested and we took so long to get there that Henry was beginning to wonder whether the Petches would be having the holiday bungalow to themselves! He was visibly relieved when we finally turned up.

Later in the '60s, when I had parted with the *Ensign* and acquired a *Renault Dauphine* – and later still a *Triumph Herald* – we had two very memorable holidays with Anne and family in a somewhat decrepit farm cottage on Anglesey. My nephew John Howard, then a schoolboy, joined us for the second of these holidays. On one of them Elizabeth was trodden on by a horse and suffered an injury to her foot. Two major events which hit the headlines during our stays on Anglesey were the Profumo affair and the Great Train Robbery, both of which happened in 1963. John Profumo was involved in a sex scandal and resigned as Secretary of State for War after admitting that he had lied to Parliament.

* * * * *

Early in 1964 I was tempted back to *Standard Triumph*, this time to be editor of the *Standard Triumph Review*, Fred Bryant who had been running the magazine since I took over from him as editor of the *Standard Triumph News* having decided to leave the company. So again I succeeded him, but only for a short time as within a month or so I had a letter from Ralph Wilson, my old chief at Ipswich, asking if I would be interested in becoming deputy editor of the *Evening Star*. It appeared that for the first time the *Star* now had its own editor and he needed a deputy.

It was a difficult decision for me to make, bearing in mind that if we moved back to East Anglia it would mean leaving Stephen and Andrew in the Midlands, and Elizabeth and Vivienne would have to change schools. This was not important as far as Vivienne was concerned but meant a major move for Elizabeth from one Grammar School to another.

At first I was undecided, spending many hours of my free time weighing up the pros and cons. In the end I plumped for the Ipswich job and a return to newspapers – much to the indignation of my boss at *Standard Triumph* (not my old one, McDonagh), who was planning for me to become involved in PR work as well as editing the magazine. It was a decision I have never regretted.

So I accepted Mr Wilson's offer and the die being cast we started making plans for our return to Ipswich after a decade in the Midlands. We had to sell our house in New Cubbington and find another to buy in Suffolk. We had no trouble at all in selling, but finding a house in the Ipswich area proved more difficult. Both Audrey and I had hoped to settle in Felixstowe, but there was nothing that we liked available in our price range. After a fruitless weekend in Ipswich, staying with Anne and Henry, we were on the point of leaving for home when Henry, who was in the estate agency business, suggested that we might be interested in a house at Needham Market that was on his books. He came with us to look at this house in Uvedale Gardens and we decided on the spot that we would have it. So in April 1964 we were to move back to Needham Market after a lapse of 18 years.

Complications again, though this time of a very different kind. Vivienne was taken ill and admitted to hospital. At first it was feared that she had developed typhoid fever for she had all the symptoms of it. Eventually, however, the doctors decided that she had contracted something similar – salmonella typhimurium. But just how and where she had picked it up no-one was ever able to discover, despite extensive inquiries by the health authorities. For six weeks Vivienne was very ill and confined to a room on her own in Warwick Hospital with Audrey by her bedside for hours on end.

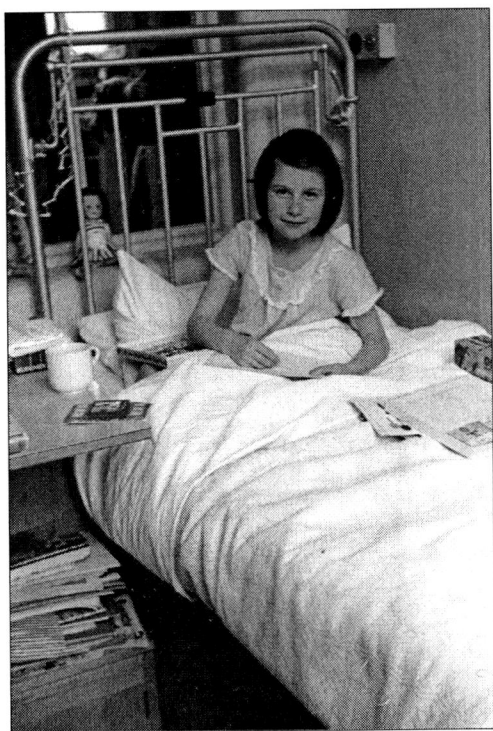

Vivienne in Warwick Hospital in 1964

Having gone to Suffolk to start my new job on the *Evening Star*, I stayed for a week or so with Audrey's mother at her house in Foxhall Road. One weekend I got time off to return to Leamington, and soon after my arrival I was told by the medical officer that I was now in quarantine and could not return to Ipswich as planned. My editor, Oscar Carter, was anything but pleased when I phoned him with the news that I wouldn't be back for at least a week, but there was nothing he could do about it.

After a week I was in fact released from quarantine and able to go back to Ipswich, leaving Audrey in the care of our neighbour, Christine Sabin, and her mother, who kindly gave Audrey a bed for the remainder of her stay in Leamington. By this time the boys, who were to stay on in the Midlands, had moved into a small flat in Warwick that Stephen had rented.

I had arranged with the headmaster of Elizabeth's school for her to be transferred to Stowmarket Grammar School, and when the day of the move came she and I travelled to Needham Market and the two of us took up residence in the Uvedale Gardens house. It fell to me therefore to take Elizabeth to be kitted out with her new school uniform at a shop in Ipswich.

When Vivienne was well enough to take the journey to Suffolk, I drove to Leamington and Audrey and I settled her as comfortably as possible for the three-hour car journey to Needham Market. Thus ended our home life in the Midlands, though with Stephen and Dot now having lived there for more than twenty years our links with Warwickshire have continued.

Return to East Anglia and the Evening Star

1964-1969

Audrey, Elizabeth and I settled in our new home, where yet again we were fortunate to have delightful next-door neighbours in Eric and Barbara Lamb, with a journalist colleague, Don Black, and his family only a few yards away. Vivienne was still recuperating, of course, and for a long time was under medical care. We paid countless visits to Ipswich Hospital, where she was a patient of Mr Mayon White. The illness had left her with a child's version of rheumatoid arthritis and a painful eye complaint, iritis, which was said to be associated with the arthritis. Her eyes were to trouble her for a long time.

Eventually Vivienne was able to start at the village primary school in Needham. A year went by before the authorities decided that she should have had a taxi for her school journeys. Too late! By this time we had decided to move her to Fonnereau House, a private day school in Ipswich, and throughout her time there I was able to convey her to and from school each day.

Back on the Star, where 'Bow' was still the chief sub-editor, I soon settled into my new job as deputy to Oscar Carter, with whom I had a good relationship. Compared with the days of 1953, when I had left the paper to go to Birmingham, the *Star* was a lot bigger in terms of the number of pages and carried new features. The sub-editing staff had also grown. The months went by without anything exceptional happening, until one day the paper was reported to the Press Council (now the Press Complaints Commission) over a front-page story about Ipswich Civic College (as it was then called). In such circumstances the editor of the paper concerned was required to submit a response to the complaint and in due course publish prominently the Press Council's adjudication.

When the day came for publication of the Press Council's findings, these upheld the complaint and criticised the *Star*. Oscar Carter duly complied and the adjudication was printed on the front page. Little did Carter realise what the effect would be: the boss, Ralph Wilson, and the other directors of the company had never been told about the complaint against the *Star* so the first they knew of it was when they read the published findings of the Press Council.

In short time Carter was summoned to Ralph Wilson's office. It was a Friday afternoon, Carter was having the weekend off and I was ready to be briefed by him about arrangements for the Saturday paper. I waited in his office – and I continued waiting, wondering what could be keeping him so long with Mr Wilson.

When he finally joined me, it was to tell me right away, "I'm finished and I'm leaving now." I could hardly believe my ears. Briefly, Oscar told me that, because he had not informed Mr Wilson or anyone else in management about the Civic College complaint right from the start, Mr Wilson had given him the option of either resigning, with immediate effect, or being sacked; he had chosen to resign.

That same afternoon Ralph Wilson sent for me and asked me to take over editorship of the *Star*, provisionally on a trial basis which he expected to confirm within a month or so. And that was how I became editor of the paper. My appointment was soon confirmed, and I held the post for nearly 14 years until my retirement in September 1978.

Oscar Carter left journalism to join the food company *Burton Son and Sanders*, where the managing director was a local MP, Keith Stainton. Initially he was a trainee in management, but we heard little more of him.

We lived in Uvedale Gardens, Needham Market, for five years, from April 1964 to March 1969. Elizabeth completed her schooling at Stowmarket Grammar in 1966, going on to Ipswich Civic College (now Suffolk College) to obtain A-levels in French and economics, while Vivienne continued at Fonnereau House School.

In the summer of 1964 Andrew, while staying with us for a week's holiday, spotted an advertisement in the *Star* for a car salesman with the *Ford* dealership *Mann Egerton* in Princes Street, Ipswich. He applied for the job, did well at the interview and was taken on. So after working out his notice at *Standard Triumph* in Coventry he returned to us at Needham to begin his (now long) career in the car sales business – and to be provided with his first car, a *Ford Anglia*. There were now five of us at home, leaving Stephen on his own in the flat at Warwick, though by this time his friendship with Dorothy Evans (Dot) had blossomed and it wasn't long before they became engaged.

It used to worry Audrey that, in moving back to East Anglia, we had abandoned the boys to their fate and uprooted Elizabeth at a particularly important time in her educational career. At the time I didn't take the same view, at least as far as Stephen and Andrew were concerned. Now I feel that, though she may have been right, the boys and Elizabeth would agree with me that in the event their lives have taken favourable courses, even if different from what might have been the case.

In February 1966 Stephen, then 22, and Dot, aged 20, were married in Warwick. My parents and Audrey's mother were there along with many other members of our respective families. Returning from their honeymoon in Paris (with about a shilling between them, I believe!) Stephen and Dot moved into a basement flat between Leamington and Warwick.

That summer Andrew accompanied his grandmother, Mrs Mead, on a holiday to Canada, where they stayed with Greta, Dennis and family. The flights were a first for both of them –

and, as it turned out, the last for Audrey's mother, who was taken ill a few months after their return and died in October 1966 as she was approaching her 79th birthday. It was a sad day for the family, and not the least for me as, from the time of our first meeting in 1940, I had become very fond of her. She was always kind to me – as was Audrey's father – and from the beginning I had felt that she encouraged our marriage.

Early in 1967 Stephen and Dot emigrated to Canada, where Stephen very quickly secured a job with *General Motors* in Toronto. It was short-lived, however, for within a few weeks he was among a large number of car workers to be made redundant as a recession hit the industry. The first opportunity that came his way was the offer of a job with *State Farm*, one of the largest American insurance companies, and, taking the plunge, he began a new career in insurance loss adjusting, his engineering experience in the motor industry standing him in good stead in dealing with that side of the business. So it was an ill wind that, in fact, did him a lot of good, leading him over the years to the top in his business life.

During the long holiday period in the summer of 1967 Elizabeth went to France as an *au pair* to a lawyer, his wife and two small children in Reims. She had secured the job through an agency in Rickmansworth, Herts, and I remember the day we took her there for the interview. My late Uncle Graham, then approaching the age of ninety, was staying with us at the time and he came, too. Not only that, but he insisted on paying for the petrol!

This was around the time – though it may have been a little later – that Andrew met his future wife, Patricia Rees. Early on in the friendship they had an evening out together and arrived at our house in Uvedale Gardens very late. Audrey and I had already retired for the night but Andrew, undeterred by that and keen to present his lady friend, got us up to be introduced. So that was our first meeting with our future daughter-in-law.

Our expanding family at Needham Market in the mid '60s
Back row: Pat, Andrew, Stephen, Dot and Elizabeth
Front row Me, Vivienne with Dixie and Audrey

A year after Stephen and Dot went to Canada Andrew joined them in London, Ontario, working as a car salesman for three months. I know that he wasn't too happy with the sales methods to which he had to adapt, but I suspect it was the parting from Pat which induced him to return to England. At any rate, after the three months he came home to us and, probably to his pleasant surprise, was soon snapped up by his old employers *Mann Egerton*. So he was back in his old job, and he and Pat became engaged in 1968.

* * * * *

In 1966 we were preparing for a big move at the office. The company's premises in Carr Street, which had been the papers' home for eighty years, with the printing works housed on the same site, were proving inadequate as the business expanded. A new site was obtained in Lower Brook Street, plans were drawn up for larger and more modern premises, a new high-speed printing press was ordered (these are usually 'made to measure') and one weekend we moved.

It was quite an achievement to print and publish from Carr Street on a Saturday afternoon and repeat the operation from Lower Brook Street in the early hours of the Monday morning! Between the two operations a mass of equipment, principally the hot metal Linotype machines, had to be partly dismantled, moved and set up in the new building. All went without a hitch. *The Green 'Un* (sports paper) was the last to be printed in Carr Street (actually in Little Colman Street, which at that time was at right angles to Carr Street and now no longer exists), and the *East Anglian Daily Times* the first off the new press in Lower Brook Street.

A year or so later there was great alarm at the new premises when fire broke out in the paper store, in which a very large number of the huge rolls of newsprint were kept. It happened late one Saturday afternoon – I think we had just printed the final edition of the *Star* – and I can see in my mind now our redoubtable chief, Ralph Wilson, rushing in to size up the situation and collaborating with the fire brigade as the rest of us evacuated the building. Although a lot of damage was done, vital equipment was saved. The press suffered the effects of the torrents of water poured on the blaze and had to be dried out. But with help from many quarters publication of the papers was not interrupted.

Andrew and Pat leaving the church with bridesmaid Elizabeth behind

By 1969 the *EADT Co.* and *Eastern Counties Newspapers* had merged, or perhaps it would be more accurate to say that the *EADT* had been absorbed by the Norwich group. There had been a strong link between the two companies for many years, with some of the Ipswich and Norwich directors sitting on the boards of both companies. At any rate, the Ipswich papers became part of the expanding Norwich group, and at about the same time big changes began to take shape in production methods – out went the hot metal Linotype machines to be replaced by the electronic photo-composition system, with paste-ups of text and pictures, and a computer base was set up at Norwich with which Ipswich was linked.

Stephen and Andrew in Canada in 1968

Stephen and Dot's house in Lucan

The switch to the new technology was not without its teething problems. But, unlike the situation which faced the national press where there was much union opposition to the new technology, the transition at Ipswich was achieved peacefully. Linotype operators were trained to operate the new kind of keyboard and soon we were all used to the different way of producing our papers. The most noticeable thing in the composing room was the big drop in the volume of noise, as the incessant clatter of the hot metal typesetting machines gave way to the almost deathly hush of the photo-composition keyboards.

All this happened in my time on the paper. Since then, of course, the wider application of computers has brought far greater changes. Today, virtually everything in the production process from the generation of reporters' copy to sub-editing and page make-up is achieved by keyboards and screens.

In the early '70s the board decided to change the *Star* from a tabloid to a broadsheet paper. It had originally been a broadsheet but changed around the time of the First World War and in the lifetime of most of its readers had been a tabloid. So this was a major change and it was left to me to design the new style paper. The reason for making the change was, as far as I can recall, to bring it into line with the broadsheet *East Anglian Daily Times*, thus assisting production. We had then reached a point where the *Star* was selling around 50,000 copies a day – its highest ever circulation – compared with the *Anglian*'s 30,000 odd. But the change didn't do the paper any good at all – readers were never happy with it and some seven years later, just before I retired, I had the job of redesigning it and turning it back into a tabloid (more about this later).

* * * * *

From our earliest days in Needham Market on returning to Suffolk from the Midlands, Audrey and I had been friendly with John and Daphne Bush who had moved to the town from the

Dunmow area of Essex. Our association came about through their daughter, Jane, who had become a friend of Elizabeth's. When she left school Jane worked for a while in Ipswich and I was able to take her in each day as well as dropping Vivienne off at her school.

At that time John Bush was working for the Milk Marketing Board and I found myself involved in more than one of his Dairy Maid contests. He later founded and ran his own frozen gateaux business for several years. I was also friendly with the general manager of the Ipswich *Regent* cinema, David Lowe, and the *Star* ran special features on many of the big stage shows at the *Regent*. One day David took me to Norwich in a vintage *Bentley* that he owned to attend the East Anglian première of the film *Born Free*.

As an editor I found myself drawn into all kinds of events and activities. At various times I made speeches about road safety, handed out awards to children who had participated in a schools' contest and judged beauty competitions. So what with producing the evening paper (not exactly by myself, of course!), writing leading articles most days and being involved in external events, there was never a dull moment. That, in truth, was the great attraction of my working life, especially in the later years, the fact that each day something different was invariably on the menu.

Elizabeth was the next of our four to leave home. After her days as an *au pair* and at the Civic College she gained entry into the service of the Foreign and Commonwealth Office. Someone from the FCO came down to the college to interview applicants and, backed by her good exam results, she was chosen for the vacant post. She had earlier considered following me into journalism but I'm sure she made the right decision. When the time came for her to go to London it happened that my sister Una, with her husband Norman and daughter Mandy, were staying with us and on the day of their return to Surrey they took Elizabeth with them and dropped her off at the hostel where she would be living – at least for a time.

Now there were four of us at Uvedale Gardens, and Vivienne and Andrew joined us on the camping expeditions we enjoyed in our new modern frame tent. This had two inner tents for sleeping with plenty of space for another camp bed as well as dining and storage areas. One weekend we went to Walberswick, near Southwold, with Anne and Henry and their boys and a friend of theirs, Joan French. Anne and Henry had their own tent and we pitched both on sand dunes close to the beach. I remember it was rather windy, obliging us to keep a close watch on the tents, frequently adjusting the guy ropes, in case they started to blow away.

I think it was in 1967 – the year after England won the World Cup by defeating Germany – that Audrey and I accompanied a party of *Evening Star* readers on a company-organised trip to Holland in the cruise ship *Franconia*. We sailed from Southampton to Rotterdam and back, spending five days enjoying the luxury provided by what had been a trans-Atlantic liner. We toured the Dutch bulb fields and the Delft china factory – and had some very late nights aboard.

It was the late nights that led to a disaster only a few hours after our return home, for the next morning, driving to the office with Vivienne beside me to be taken to school, I must have been so tired that as we went down Henley Road in Ipswich, with Christchurch Park on our left and Ipswich School on our right, I momentarily dropped off to sleep.

The first I knew of any danger was when Vivienne shouted, "Look out, Dad," but it was too late to prevent an accident.

Early summer 1969 at Felixstowe with Anne's family
From left: Anne with Christopher and Nicholas, Pat, Audrey,
Andrew, Vivienne with Dixie, Elizabeth and Henry

Happy camping days
Vivienne and Elizabeth with Anne and Audrey inside the tent

Although I 'came to' quickly and 'stood on the brakes' I couldn't stop before crashing into a car left against the nearside kerb while its owner was taking his dog for a walk in the park – and we weren't wearing seatbelts.

Poor Vivienne's head shattered the windscreen – it was years before the last piece of glass was removed from her face – and she fractured her left wrist. I was crushed by the steering wheel, so my sternum (chest bone) was broken. We ended up in Ipswich Hospital, the one then sited in Anglesea Road, and were kept in for several days in different wards. I was away from the office for a month. What the dog owner had to say when he returned to his badly damaged car, I never did know. Andrew, already at work in his Princes Street showroom, soon heard about a damaged *Morris 1100* being taken by transporter to another garage, put two and two together, suspecting that we could have been involved in an accident, and quickly had his fears confirmed. My brother-in-law, Henry, also spotted the damaged car on the transporter.

The irony of it was that the seatbelts which would have saved us, or at least minimised our injuries, were hanging in our garage at home. I had removed them from the *Triumph Herald* but hadn't got round to fitting them in the *Morris* when I changed cars. At that time the fitting and wearing of seat belts, though strongly recommended, was not compulsory. An object lesson here.

The Move to Felixstowe and Travel Abroad

1969-1974

The late '60s saw us on the move again – this time to Felixstowe, where we had wanted to settle in the first place. In late 1968 we heard of homes being built in the Old Felixstowe area of Ferndown Road lying between High Road East and Colneis Road. A semi-detached bungalow then in the early stages of construction was available and we jumped at the chance of buying it. We put the Uvedale Gardens house on the market and found a buyer in a retired spinster then living on the coast.

March 1969 found us moving into the newly-built bungalow – that is, Audrey and myself along with Andrew and Vivienne. Audrey and I were to live there for the next 15 years and 8 months, among many friends old and new. Yet again we were fortunate to find ourselves next door to charming people, an elderly couple, Keith and Eileen Bowman. Eileen had been a teacher at Felixstowe Ladies' College (which now, sadly, is no more) and Keith had been in public relations at the noted agricultural firm, *Ransomes, Sims and Jefferies*. It was through the Bowmans that I came to attend sessions of Felixstowe Debating Society, where I got to know many more interesting people.

Among the old friendships which we actively renewed was that with Keith and Dorrie Wood and their daughter, Judith. Audrey had known them since her childhood days, maintaining over the years a special friendship with Dorrie's sister, Olive, today a widow living in Cheddar. Keith has had a distinguished career in electronics – he was involved in the development of radar at

Bawdsey, worked on automatic landing systems at Martlesham, oversaw atomic weapons testing at Orfordness and, in later years, became a consultant to the Federation of Electronic Engineers. He was awarded the OBE in 1979, and commuted from Felixstowe to his office in London until his retirement in 2002 – at the age of 87! Judith has not allowed a physical handicap to stop her from using her talents and she has served on several committees in Felixstowe.

Not long after our move into Ferndown Road my father, whose health had deteriorated considerably over the previous year or so, died at home in Manor Gardens, Guildford. He had reached the age of 78 a few weeks earlier. My mother had nursed him for the last several months, having his bed moved to the ground floor. As an only child he had had a very protected upbringing, and he had lost his first wife when he was only 28. Mixed fortunes followed: he became very deaf and he wasn't very good at handling financial matters. But he had great charm and a wonderful sense of humour, as my sister-in-law, Anne, and her husband, Henry, will confirm in recalling times when he visited them on business trips to Ipswich.

Not long afterwards Mother moved into a bungalow near Bunty and Arthur in Onslow Village, Guildford; it was Arthur, in fact, who was instrumental in getting the bungalow for her.

Moving on to May of 1969 we come to Andrew's marriage to Pat. The wedding took place in Ipswich at a church near the bride's parents' home, and there was a last-minute hitch when the taxi which had been ordered for the bride failed to make an appearance. Hurried consultations resulted in a relative of Pat's driving her to the church in his *Triumph Herald* – twenty minutes late. On returning from their honeymoon Andrew and Pat rented a static caravan on a site off Foxhall Road (shades of Audrey and myself!) before, a few months later, buying their first house in Defoe Road.

*My parents in Guildford in the garden of their home in the
early '60s*

In the summer of that year we ventured further afield with our
tent. Taking Vivienne with us, we went to a site at Wells on the
north Norfolk coast, arriving in a rainstorm. I shall never forget
putting the tent up in the rain and trying to keep our luggage
and bedding dry. We didn't like the site anyway and moved to a
smaller one at Holme-next-Sea further along the coast, though
the weather was not much better there. This was in July 1969
and on the 28th of that month our first grandchild, Jenalynn,
was born in London, Ontario. Knowing that we were on
holiday somewhere, Stephen rang Andrew with the news – but
how were we to be told that we had become grandparents? I
think Andrew did a bit of detective work to find out exactly
where we were and got a message through to the camp site.
Meanwhile, we had gone into Hunstanton to call on Audrey's

brother Jack, and José, who were then living there. Taking pity on us in our watery state, they insisted that we stay with them for the night. (I am writing this, by the way, eleven days after the birth of my first *great*-grandchild, Elliemay Audrey Ancliff, whose mother Jenalynn is now approaching her 33rd birthday).

The '70s were eventful years for us, with marriages, births and a death in the family, inter-continental comings and goings, Stephen and Dot's eventual settlement back in England and Elizabeth's in Norway, the start of Vivienne's life as a diplomatic wife, my association with the Guild of British Newspaper Editors and Audrey and I going to the guild's splendid annual conferences, developments in printing techniques, the reconversion of the *Evening Star* into a tabloid, and my retirement as the paper's editor towards the end of the decade. It was also a period during which Audrey, for the first time in her life, took on spells of (part-time) employment.

Through all these years there were political changes and other historic events, including the election of Margaret Thatcher as Britain's first woman Prime Minister, the American landing on the moon and, nearer home, the rapid expansion of the docks at Felixstowe.

Audrey and I not only enjoyed life beside the sea but trailed our caravans (four in all) to various parts of the country. And in all these years we had with us the dear little Jack Russell, Dixie, that we had acquired from the RSPCA when we lived at Needham Market. We also had a budgerigar, Timmy, who had been part of the household since our days at Sutton Coldfield. We usually took Dixie with us on our caravan holidays and left Timmy with my mother in Guildford.

Dixie, aged about two when she came to us, lived on for a further 16 years. Taken ill when we were in Scotland, she somehow survived the long journey home – we stopped off twice for vets to give her injections – but to our great sorrow we had to have her put down the next day. Timmy had what appeared to be a stroke when we were away on holiday and Dot was keeping house for us, and died at the ripe old age – for a budgie – of 13.

* * * * *

I had become a member of the Guild of British Newspaper Editors soon after the merger of the Ipswich and Norwich papers and for some years I was the region's secretary-treasurer. Audrey and I enjoyed several annual conferences – at Bournemouth, Bath, Harrogate, Cardiff, Chester and Liverpool. Elizabeth joined us for a ladies' day at Colchester and Vivienne was with us for the Bournemouth conference. It was in fact through these guild get-togethers that Audrey and I formed a close relationship with Cliff and Audrey Butler. Sad to say Cliff died in the '80s a little more than a year after retiring from the editorship of the Norwich weekly series of papers. Our – lately, my – warm friendship with Audrey Butler continues to this day and we exchange visits.

Compared with Carr Street days both the *Anglian* and the *Star*, and the company's weekly series, developed considerably right from the start of the move to Lower Brook Street. By the '70s the editorial staff had grown: Alan Everett was in charge of the sports department, Henry Clark of photographic, Geoff Harvey, a veteran journalist who had earlier had a career at sea, continued as chief reporter, and Frank Tonkinson – 'Tonky' – was news editor. There were many more sub-editors. For a time Elizabeth Sinclair, who had become a sub-editor in the days when it was rare to find women doing such work and even female reporters were thin on the ground, held the job of chief sub when Alfred Bowden ('Bow') retired. She was succeeded by Mike Read, who later moved to the *BBC* at Norwich and was in turn succeeded by Rodney Kiddell. 'Rod' became my deputy and took over editorship of the *Star* when I retired.

Reporters worked for both the *Anglian* and the *Star*, but we had our own staff of feature writers. Among them were Victoria Ainsworth, who was also the paper's motoring writer (I learnt that she died early in 2002); Derek Booth, who later went to live in the United States; Elizabeth Grice, who has for several years been a feature writer on *The Daily Telegraph*; and Bob Malster, later to become the author of several books on Suffolk, Felixstowe in particular. All of them shared with me, at different times, the task of writing leaders each day. A character among the reporting staff was Margaret Warren – I'd describe her as a kind of Margaret Thatcher type! When 'Tonky' retired he was succeeded as news editor by Reg Hardy, and in due course Henry Clark handed over as picture editor to John Loughton.

With the continuing developments in printing we began to experiment with 'spot' colour. Colour is used so much today that one tends to forget that newspapers used to be 'black and white only' – and not so very long ago either. On reflection I am sure our early efforts were rather feeble, but at least we were moving in the right direction. We had reached the stage of receiving black and white pictures from the Press Association in London by electronic means, whereas in earlier years we had to send someone to the railway station to collect prints arriving by train. I remember the day the Americans landed men on the moon and we set up a camera to take pictures of this historic event as they were televised – pictures which we printed on the *Star*'s front page.

The growth of Felixstowe docks often made the headlines. Luckily for us we had a lively shipping reporter, Don Black, who had many useful contacts. Incidentally, it was through the foresight of a Cornishman named Trelawny that the docks really took off, eventually becoming Britain's largest container port, aided by the dockers in London and Liverpool who saw containerisation as a threat to their jobs and resisted the change. Felixstowe knew better.

Family-wise (to use an apt but ugly term) we went through very busy and rewarding years. Vivienne had left Fonnereau House School not long after our move from Needham Market and completed her education at Deben High in Felixstowe. At 17 she left school and entered a commercial college. At 18 she passed her driving test and worked for a year in an Ipswich branch of *Barclays Bank* before going to Canada to stay with Stephen and Dot for three months. On her return she took an *au pair* job in Jersey where the parents of the one child she had gone to look after made excessive use of her: she had to deliver cars and flowers, haul sacks of potatoes up into a loft, do all the washing and ironing (the machine was out of action) and was regarded as a general factotum. After that it was a 21-month stint as a receptionist at Felixstowe's *Marlborough Hotel*, using a second-hand *Hillman Imp* that I had bought for Audrey to get to work and back. Her next move was to Norway, where initially she stayed with Elizabeth.

And as that brings me to Elizabeth we'll take up her career. After a time working for the Foreign Office in London she decided to try her luck in Canada, joining Stephen and Dot for a while until she not only got herself a job but found a flat to share with another English girl in Toronto. While in Canada she actually had two jobs, the second being with a radio station. A couple of years later she and her friend, Josie, decided to return to Britain but to make an extensive tour of Canada and the United States first. So across Canada they went, then down the west coast of America and into Mexico, and back to Toronto up the east coast of the United States. I fear that their adventures – and they had some – will have to be the subject of another book, perhaps by Elizabeth!

Back in London, she rejoined the Foreign Office and was given specialised training before being posted to Oslo. And it was there that she met Lars Fuglesang and where Vivienne, who had taken a temporary job as housekeeper to a Norwegian divorcee, met Peter Broom who, like Elizabeth, was on the staff at the British Embassy.

Vivienne with Elizabeth during a more recent visit to Norway

* * * * *

Meanwhile Audrey and I were living very happily in Ferndown Road. Audrey, feeling that she wanted to do something apart from running the house and looking after me, joined the meals-on-wheels service in Felixstowe. Each week she would go round in another lady's car and call on elderly people to deliver their meals; if her driver was away, I stepped into the breach whenever possible and we did the round together in our car. Audrey delivered most of the meals but I did some and used to help with the washing up (no machine) at the end of the run.

Audrey also worked behind the counter at a chemist's in the town – that was in fact the first paid job she'd ever had – and it was there that she met and formed a lifelong friendship with Barbara Davies (now Barbara Johnson). The chemist himself was a friend of the sister, Phyllis, of Audrey's sister-in-law José, and Phyllis did the shop's accounts. A few years later, having left the chemist's, Audrey worked in a tiny kiosk where sweets and cigarettes were sold. At both places she found that she could deal with sales and manage the change, though she had been somewhat apprehensive to start with – needlessly so, I used to tell her.

About the mid-'70s I persuaded Audrey to have driving lessons. Again, she was rather apprehensive but she persevered, even though she didn't get on very well with her male instructor, and I acquired the *Hillman Imp* for her as an inducement. This was later to be succeeded by a *Triumph Herald,* which Audrey didn't like at all. Sadly, she failed her driving test – I believe something went wrong at a roundabout. She restarted tuition with another instructor, a lady this time with a smaller car, and had she kept this up she would, I'm sure, have passed the test in the end. But family affairs were crowding in on her – two weddings were on the horizon, Stephen and Dot were with us with Jenalynn and Tracy, born in 1971, and Charlotte, too, was about to be born. So she gave up driving, and I have always blamed myself for not persuading her to get back to it later on when there were no distractions.

Going back to 1971: this was the year when Audrey and I, with Vivienne, went to Canada for the first time. Stephen and Dot were then living in Lucan, a small township a few miles from London, Ontario, where Stephen worked. Tracy had been born in the March and during our visit in the summer she was baptized in the local church. Getting to Canada economically wasn't so easy then as it is today. The cheap flights were by charter and to qualify as a passenger one had to belong to an approved organisation. Ours was the British-Canadian Families' Association and we had to attend its meetings in Ipswich for a certain period.

The day finally came when we secured our places on a flight from Gatwick to Toronto – our first flight together. The fare was £50 return, which would be extraordinarily cheap today but was still quite a lot for us in 1971. I know that Audrey saved money from her job at the chemist's and paid her own fare.

Two or three years later Audrey and I went to Canada again for Christmas with Stephen and Dot at their new home in London, Ontario. Bunty and Arthur travelled with us and stayed with Bunty's son, Robin, and his wife, Barbara, in Burlington, about fifty miles from Toronto.

Whereas we had had very hot weather on our first visit we were now experiencing the rigours of a Canadian winter: snow lay deep everywhere, the temperature was well below zero and some of the smaller lakes were frozen over. Nevertheless we enjoyed a typical Canadian Christmas.

On both visits to Canada we went to see Greta, Dennis and family at Newmarket some thirty miles from Toronto. I remember Dennis taking us to Lake Simcoe during our winter visit and seeing anglers drilling through the ice to lower their lines into the water beneath. It was quite safe to drive vehicles on to the frozen lake and many people did just that.

In contrast, during our first stay, at Lucan, we all went up to the north of Ontario, in the area of Parry Sound, with a trailer tent. The sand on the beach of the lake was far too hot to stand on with bare feet and wooded areas were alive with mosquitoes. While at Greta's we drove to Niagara Falls, one of the most spectacular sights in the world.

On a beautiful summer's day in June 1972 we celebrated Audrey's 50th birthday at Woburn Abbey. We went to the stately home for the day with Andrew, Pat and Vivienne, touring the house itself, the spacious grounds and that part of the estate where wild animals were able to roam at will. As we drove through the park the curiosity of the monkeys led them to jump on to the bonnet of our car and attempt to wrench off the windscreen wipers! On our way home we stopped off for a meal at St Neots; Vivienne, I remember, wasn't happy with the food – but the rest of us enjoyed it.

In 1974 Audrey and I paid our first visit to Norway to stay with Elizabeth and to meet Lars. Through our shipping reporter, Don Black's, contacts at the docks we were able to get passages in a cargo ship plying between Felixstowe and Scandinavia. I think our return fares came to only £70! The ship was the *Valerie,* whose captain, named Screetch, made us very welcome, providing us with a comfortable cabin and even putting a bottle of whisky on the table ready for our arrival. We had meals with Captain Screetch and his ship's officers, as did another couple from Harwich who sailed with us as far as Denmark. They were in fact on their honeymoon – after living together for twenty years before the bridegroom, who had been married previously, was free to marry.

Captain Screetch himself was a 'larger-than-life' character. I can see him now, taking the ship out of dock by manipulating the controls with his feet from an open end of the bridge, and he was the life and soul of the parties we had in the evenings. A less exuberant captain, though a very pleasant man, took over for our return sailing. The last I heard of Captain Screetch he was master of a ship in the Middle East.

The most memorable part of our voyage to Norway was the final leg sailing the fifty or so miles up Oslo Fjord with its breathtaking scenery on either side and masses of small islands, many with little houses on them. As we approached Oslo itself we could see most of the city – it is small as capitals go – spread out from the heights of Holmenkollen with its impressive Olympic ski jump, down to the waterfront with its fortress and twin-towered City Hall – a truly magnificent sight. And on the quayside in the area where cargo ships docked stood Elizabeth beside the *Mini* she'd had shipped out from England, waiting to welcome us to Norway.

An official came aboard to check our passports and ensure that we had 'nothing to declare' and we were soon in the *Mini* speeding to Elizabeth's flat. That same evening we were introduced to Lars. We watched from a window of the flat as he parked his *VW Beetle* in the street below and in no time at all our future son-in-law had us in his car for a tour of the city.

Another overseas trip for us both, very different in nature, was a five-day visit to Moscow. This was organised by Scope, an *Evening Star* club for women, which had attracted quite a substantial membership and was arranging regular events. The Moscow trip, on a larger scale than previous excursions, proved a great success and Audrey and I personally rated it our most interesting holiday.

In the mid-1970s the Communist Party was in full control of the Soviet Union, so it really was quite an event for us to go behind the Iron Curtain to see for ourselves, as far as we were permitted, what life was like under a dictatorship. We stayed in a skyscraper hotel, on the 19th floor, and did the 'rounds' of Moscow, visiting the famous circus and the ballet, the space museum where the first Russian sputniks were displayed, and the Hall of Congresses, a building with an enormous auditorium where Communist conferences were held. We travelled on the immaculately kept underground and rode through the snow in a troika. We had to be well wrapped up against the intense cold – many degrees below zero.

There wasn't a lot to buy, though the Russian people formed long queues outside the shops. Clothing was very expensive for them. In Red Square we visited Lenin's tomb. Armed guards stood by as we passed into the chamber where the dictator's embalmed body lay. Then we went on to the noted *GUM* store, a huge building with avenues of shops on two levels and nothing like a western department store.

One day our party was taken to a government building where we, and other tourists, sat round tables and were invited to put questions to a top table of officials. I couldn't resist the opportunity! Why, I asked, was the Soviet Government still keeping Rudolf Hess, by then a very sick man, in captivity in Berlin nearly thirty years after the war ended? The answer came swiftly: because the Germans killed up to 20 million Russians and the people remembered that, holding Hess largely responsible. Hess, who was Hitler's deputy, has since died.

After we visited the circus one member of our party, a little lady from Norwich who was proud of her Communist links in Britain and probably felt as though she was in Heaven in Moscow, got left behind when we boarded our coach. Fortunately, a young man she approached spoke a little English and he kindly took her to the underground and escorted her to the door of our hotel. Earlier in this book I told how I was once a 'little boy lost' in London. Now we had a 'little lady lost' in Moscow, as I related in an *Evening Star* full-page feature about our trip as soon as we got home!

The '70s saw much thought given to the question of constructing a by-pass round Ipswich and providing a new crossing of the River Orwell to cope with the ever-increasing volume of traffic to and from Felixstowe docks. Both the *Anglian* and the *Star* weighed in with ideas and comments on the various proposals put forward.

At the *Star* we were particularly interested in the idea of an immersed tube tunnel as a means of crossing the river, as we felt at the time that a tunnel rather than a bridge would be less harmful to the landscape. With one of my feature writers I attended a London meeting of engineers who were behind this idea. But it was not to be: the final decision was that a bridge should be built, and I must say now that it was right, for the beautiful structure, nearly a mile long, that spans the Orwell has proved not only adequate for the huge amount of traffic it is called on to carry every day but, far from spoiling the estuary landscape, has added to its attraction. So, while we at the *Star* may have lost the day, we had no regrets when the graceful bridge was finally opened.

Meanwhile great strides were made in rerouting parts of the A45 (since redesignated the A14) as a dual carriageway to provide, as it does today, a through-route from Felixstowe to the M6 in the Midlands of almost motorway standard. In earlier days our journey from Ipswich to the Midlands took us on the old roads through the towns of Needham Market, Stowmarket, Bury St Edmunds, Newmarket, Eaton Socon and Bedford, and on to the M1 at Newport Pagnell, then on the M45 to Coventry. Today it's a straight run without touching any towns at all.

During construction of the A14 in Suffolk a lot of the sand and gravel needed was extracted from large fields alongside the railway line at Needham Market, leaving what is now Bosmere Lake in an attractively landscaped recreational area. In the days when we lived in Uvedale Gardens, and the lake had yet to be formed, I used to take Dixie for walks there.

In the mid-'70s meetings were held with the aim of establishing a talking newspaper for the visually handicapped in the Ipswich area. I was in on this project from the outset and became the first editor of Sound On, as the newspaper was named. Material was taken from daily issues of the East Anglian Daily Times and the Evening Star, edited and then recorded by a small team of readers on audio tapes which were distributed to those wishing to take this service. Sound On has flourished and a year or so ago I attended a get-together to celebrate its 25th anniversary.

The Orwell Bridge under construction in the '80s

Audrey with Audrey Butler at Pin Mill, Suffolk in 1988

Stephen with Jenalynn and Tracy in the mid-'70s

Weddings, more Grandchildren and Retirement

1975-1979

Into 1975 and at home we were planning for Elizabeth's wedding on 23rd August, with an expected influx of visitors from overseas: Stephen and Dot with Jenalynn and Tracy, and Greta and Dennis were coming from Canada, and members of Lars' family as well as Vivienne, from Norway. What we didn't know was that Stephen would be giving up his job and that he and Dot planned to set up home in England, though we did know, of course, that Charlotte was expected to be born in January 1976.

The wedding was memorable on two counts: Lars' mother, sister and little niece all wore colourful Norwegian national dress, and after the ceremony at the church in Old Felixstowe the reception was held at the historic *Seckford Hall* with its beautiful garden.

It is worth recording that at a late stage in making the wedding arrangements Lars had to switch his best man when his friend Erik Holtedahl was forced to withdraw. Erik was working in Moscow and had married a Russian girl, Aljona, but the authorities would not let his wife leave the country to attend the wedding. So Lars' twin brother, Christian, performed the duties of best man. Much later Aljona was given permission to leave the Soviet Union and she and Erik settled in Norway. They now live in Oslo, and on a recent visit I not only met them at a party on an island in Oslo Fjord but, with Elizabeth, had lunch with Aljona at her home.

Elizabeth and Lars' wedding at Old Felixstowe Church
Lillemor Fugelesang, Lars, Elizabeth, Lise and Kari Lise

The 'Mead' siblings in the grounds of Seckford Hall
Anne, Jack, Brenda, Audrey, Bernard, Greta, Marjorie, Kaye

Vivienne and Peter became engaged in 1975 and were planning to be married in February 1976 in the same church in Old Felixstowe. It fell to my lot to see Mr Bunn, proprietor of *Seckford Hall*, again to book the hotel for a second time. Jokingly, I asked Mr Bunn if I would get a discount for wedding reception No.2. He had an instant reply: "I'm afraid not, but if you want to book a third, you can have it free," knowing full well that I had only two daughters!

It was on St Valentine's Day, 14th February, in 1976 that Vivienne and Peter were married, and though it was winter time the setting of *Seckford Hall* was ideal for the occasion. Again, there was a large family gathering.

The two weddings over, Elizabeth and Lars and Vivienne and Peter were back in Oslo while Stephen and Dot, with their girls, had settled in with us in Ferndown Road. Two days after Vivienne's wedding Stephen went into 'digs' in Tunbridge Wells, having been working for a loss-adjusting company since his return from Canada. A month or so later he and Dot moved into a house of their own at Braintree. It was during their 15 months there that Dot's father died, not very long after his retirement.

By 1977 both Stephen and Dot were somewhat disillusioned with life back in England, Stephen because his job did not come up to expectations and Dot (I think) because she missed Canada and all that it offered. At any rate, they decided to sell up and return to Canada. Though Audrey and I understood how they felt, we were saddened to lose them from our shores again. Little did we then know what the future held and that within two years they would be back in England, this time for good – at least, as I write these lines in September 2002!

In Canada they moved into a house in Windsor, Ontario, with Detroit just across the water, and Stephen resumed loss adjusting work with another employer. Audrey and I never visited Windsor, though on one of our two visits to Canada Stephen took us to the huge motor museum at Detroit.

Before the '70s were out our tally of grandchildren had risen to six: Victoria had been born in 1974 and Charlotte in 1976: next came Sarah in 1977 and Emma in 1979 – and there were seven more to come!

Andrew holding baby Sarah, and Victoria

* * * * *

Back to the newspapers: by 1978 the *EADT* management had decided that the *Evening Star* should be returned to tabloid format – a decision that I know pleased our readers. So once more my staff and I had the job of redesigning the paper. In its new form it was quite different from the tabloid of old.

With bound copies of the Evening Star 1965-1978

Time with the *Evening Star* was running out for me with the approach of retirement on my 62nd birthday in September. But we managed to have everything ready for the appearance of the new paper eleven days beforehand, so I was able to press the button for the first run. Only about a dozen more leaders to write before I would hand over to my successor as editor, Rodney Kiddell. The Evening Star of today is, again, a different paper – it would indeed be most surprising if it were to look anything like the last one I edited nearly a quarter of a century ago. Newspaper tastes and styles are forever changing. Not only that but technological advances make it possible for presentation to be far more colourful than what it used to be in the days of 'hot metal' production. The Star has won several awards in recent years.

A month or so before my retirement there was a great day for Ipswich, for the Star and for me, when the Town won the FA Cup in the final against Arsenal at Wembley. As ever, the Star had strongly supported the Town and we were closely involved in the celebrations when many thousands of people packed the Cornhill and surrounding streets to express their delight. The team, led by the captain, Mick Mills, and the manager, Bobby Robson, came out on the balcony of the Town Hall – and I was fortunate to be among them. It really was a memorable day for us all.

Within weeks came another memorable time for me in more ways than one. It started with a presentation at a board meeting in Norwich, then came another presentation at the office when I handed over the reins to Rodney Kiddell, and finally a retirement party for me, given by the company, at the *Great White Horse Hotel*. But just before that I was in for a great surprise: all the family had been invited to the party and I knew that Andrew and Pat and Elizabeth and Lars would be there.

Vivienne and Peter were in Saudi Arabia so I realised that they would not be able to come, and that, I thought, also applied to Stephen and Dot in far-off Canada.

So when, shortly before my last day at the office, the phone rang and a receptionist said that my son had called to see me, I told her to send him up, naturally expecting Andrew to appear. Instead, a smiling Stephen presented himself! He had flown over for the occasion and, at the same time, to engage in talks with his former boss, Derek Fisher, at *Hammond and Fisher*, about a possible return to Britain to join him in a partnership to run the company (Hammond had severed his connection with it, leaving Fisher at the helm). I hadn't known about this possibility: in the event Stephen and Dot did return, a year later, in October 1979, and Stephen joined Derek Fisher.

Elizabeth and Lars didn't have to come from Norway for my party as they had earlier moved to England when Lars took up a position with the Norwegian company Norsk Hydro at their Feltham office.

It might be thought that as I had had such an interesting job for so many years I would perhaps find retirement a problem. Not a bit of it! From Day One I was as happy in retirement as I had been working. In fact, for short periods over the next six years I was employed by the National Council for the Training of Journalists. At various times I travelled to London, Epping, Hastings, Croydon, Portsmouth, Cardiff, Bristol, Rugby and Norwich for duties such as instructing on sub-editing courses, interviewing potential trainees, validating course work and generally being involved in the training and examination of young journalist entrants at colleges and training centres.

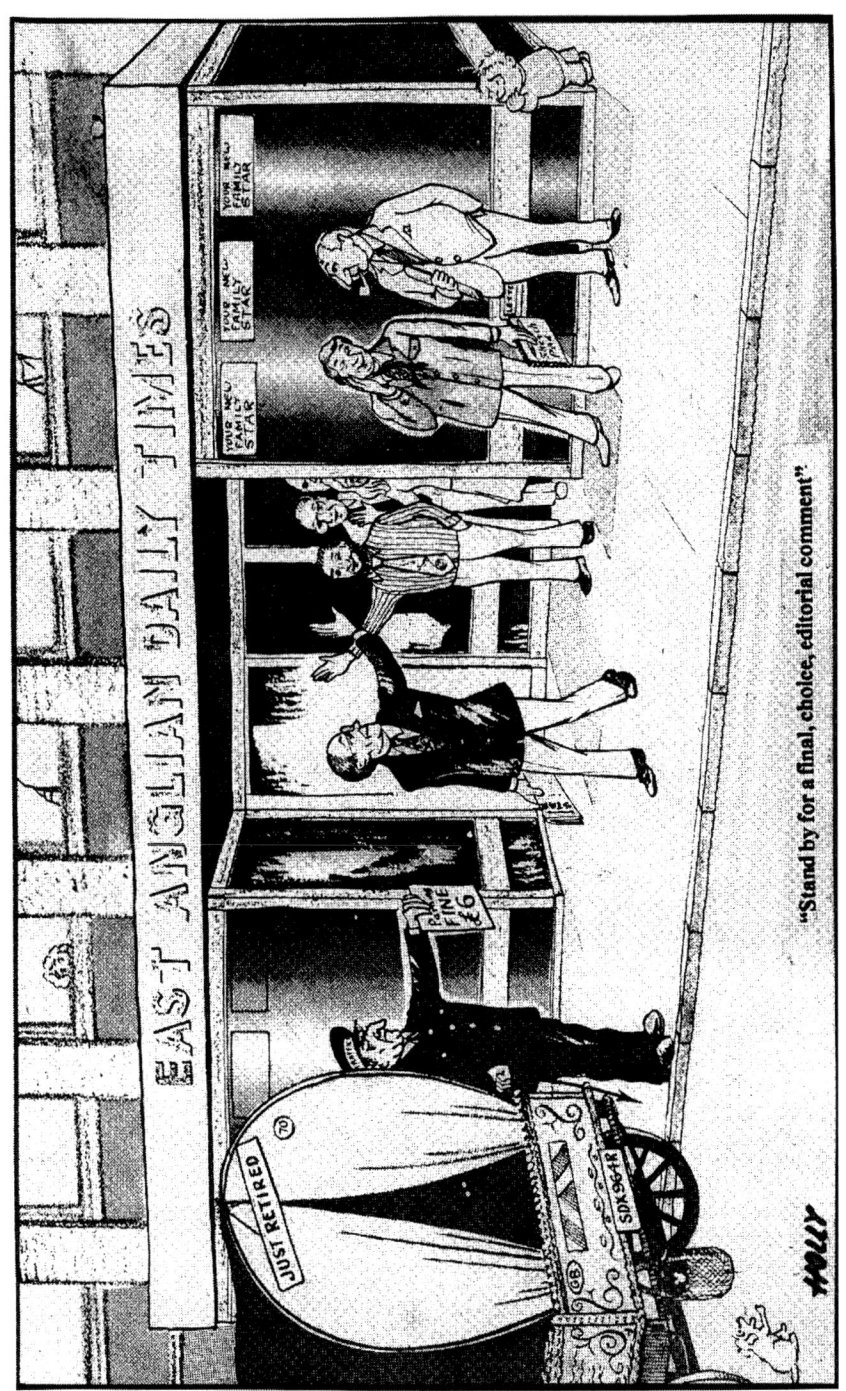

"Stand by for a final, choice, editorial comment".

HOLLY

In January 1979 my mother died while staying with Una at Godalming, three months short of her 80th birthday. Audrey and I had spent the Christmas of 1978 with Elizabeth and Lars at their house in Weybridge, and Vivienne and Peter were there, too, having come home on leave from Saudi Arabia. So we had all been able to see my mother during her last days at her home in Guildford.

We Settle in Waldringfield and Revisit Normandy

1980-1999

The '80s were fruitful years within the family, with the birth of Fredrik in London in 1980, Thomas in Norway the following year, (Elizabeth and Lars having returned to the Oslo area by then), Jessica also in 1981, William in 1984, Annie in 1985 and Sophie in 1988. Audrey and I now had twelve grandchildren, bringing the total of family members, including ourselves, to twenty-two.

Here I am with seven of our grandchildren

L to R: Thomas, William, Emma, Jessica, Annie, Fredrik and Sophie

There were more departures, too: Audrey's sister Brenda died in 1983, Marjorie's husband Leonard in 1984, Una's Norman and David, Brenda's second husband, both in 1985. Audrey and I drove to Surrey for Norman's funeral the day before we flew to Swaziland to stay with Vivienne and Peter. So while our immediate family was growing, the older generation in the wider family was declining in numbers – as one would expect, of course.

We were now in the Thatcher years, the 'Iron Lady' having become Britain's first woman Prime Minister in May 1979. She was to 'reign' for the next eleven years.

In 1981 there was a national census and I was one of Felixstowe's enumerators. The job, lasting about a fortnight, involved delivering census forms to a large number of homes in the town and collecting them some days later. I have never knocked on so many doors or seen the inside of so many houses and flats in my life! In some cases it was necessary to help the occupant to fill in the forms and if people were out I would have to call a second or even a third time. But it was an interesting experience and I was paid about £150. By the time the next census came round I was too old to take part.

By 14th March 1982 Audrey and I had been married for 40 years and to celebrate this Ruby Anniversary we had a family party at the *Belstead Brook Hotel* in Ipswich. All our children were there and little Emma, then not yet 3 years old and wearing a red velvet dress with a white collar, stepped forward to present Audrey with a posy of flowers.

During the early '80s we were considering making a move. This time Audrey was the one with the itchy feet and she persuaded me that we should look around for a place in the country. We didn't take the idea all that seriously at first, and, anyway, the houses that we did look at, in places ranging from Stutton, near Ipswich, and villages in the Bury St Edmunds area and North Suffolk not far from Southwold, didn't appeal to us at all. Then, one day in the summer of 1984 I happened to be looking through the housing ads. in the *Anglian* while we were having breakfast and spotted something which had immediate appeal – it was an ad. for a converted school house. I sent for the details and when these came we lost no time in driving the short distance to Waldringfield, where we easily found the house in question. A phone call to the agents, whose representative came over from Woodbridge right away, and we were inside the house which was to become our new home for a longer period than anywhere else we had lived since our marriage way back in 1942. We were told that we would have to make a quick decision as other parties were interested in the property (sales talk?), and we did just that after a second inspection the same evening.

Though we liked Felixstowe and had long associations with the town, we never had any regrets about our decision to move, in November 1984, to the delightful village beside the Deben, and into *The Old School House* where I am writing now in the autumn of 2002.

Earlier in 1984 Audrey and I enjoyed a long trip by car across Northern Europe. We had both wanted to visit the beaches and battlefields in those areas where I had been from 1944 to 1946: at the same time Elizabeth had invited us to stay in Norway for two or three weeks. So off we went in our *Capri* to Dover and over to Calais and then on into Normandy. We stayed firstly in Bayeux, then at a private house in a village near Mont Pincon, the scene of much fighting in 1944. In the few days we were in Normandy, we went to the beach at Arromanches where I had landed and to several places where fierce battles had taken place before the breakout and push across France, among them Villers Bocage, Tilly-sur-Seulles and Aunay-sur-Odon, as well as the outskirts of Caen. At the British cemetery in Bayeux I found the grave of my friend, Geoff Goom, killed before the breakout from the bridgehead.

***At the grave of my RTR comrade Geoff Goom
killed near Caen in June 1944***

From Normandy we drove across Northern France into Belgium and Holland and then on into Germany, following my wartime route as far as possible. We spent a night in Cambrai, scene of the battle in 1916 when British tanks made their first appearance, then a night with my niece, Valerie, and Michael, at the Army base at Rheindahlen, and another at Itzehoe, north of Hamburg, where I had found myself when the war ended in May 1945, before going on to Puttgarten to get the ferry to Rødby in Denmark. A drive northwards and through Copenhagen in a thunderstorm took us to Helsingor, where we stayed in a log cabin for the night.

Next morning it was another short ferry crossing to Helsingborg in Sweden. Then we drove the final 300 miles up the west coast of Sweden into Norway, through Oslo and to Elizabeth's at Billingstad. The complete drive took us just over a week and we wished afterwards that we had spent longer in Normandy, though we were to visit the battlefields a second time, and I went a third time with Stephen and Andrew. After a relaxing week or so at Elizabeth's, we drove to Gothenburg for the return journey to England on the ferry to Harwich.

The move – it was to be our last – to Waldringfield on 19th November 1984 went smoothly. I remember that Audrey's brother Jack came over from Wickham Skeith with José and helped me to fix the new electric cooker that we had bought. Within a week or two we had made arrangements for a better heating system to be installed and some work done outside: a walled bank was made and a wide farm gate put up, whilst the ground leading to the entrance door was shingled and conifers were planted to mark the boundary on the north side. Later on we had a glazed porch built and the back garden, somewhat neglected till then, was grassed over after a large tree had been felled. After the gales of October 1987 and another storm which hit East Anglia about a year later, a very tall beech tree quite close to the bungalow looked so dangerous that I obtained permission for it to be cut down. We had already improved the garden by having a paved patio laid. This adjoined two unsightly sheds standing side by side, which, much to Audrey's relief, we eventually had removed to make way for a summer house – a gift from Stephen.

Those fearsome gales of 1987 which caused so much damage in Western, Southern and South-eastern England, left their mark on Waldringfield too. I remember that weekend very well for we were booked on a flight to Finland to stay with Elizabeth and Lars (they lived just outside Helsinki for six years). The hurricane-force winds tore across the country during the night of Friday 17th October, killing 17 people and leaving a £300-million trail of destruction from Cornwall to East Anglia. In the morning we went outside to view the damage: our TV aerial on its pole had been completely wrecked and lay on the ground, and a tall tree just outside the boundary of our property had been uprooted, fortunately falling into the adjoining wood, its extensive roots having pushed one of our sheds up in the air to a height of about four feet!

Before leaving for Finland that weekend we joined a family party at Bernard's at Wickham Skeith on the Saturday evening, and it was as we set off that we found the winding road out of the village blocked by more fallen trees. We got through by driving up a bank and along the edge of a field, then down again when the road was clear. At Bernard's the evening party went ahead by the light of oil lamps and candles, the storm having cut off the power supply, as indeed it had at Waldringfield and many other places. We got back home with some difficulty, again negotiating the obstructions in the road into Waldringfield.

The aftermath of the gales in October 1987

Next day, or it may have been on the Monday, we went off to Heathrow to catch our plane, passing widespread damage *en route*, and it was not until we returned from Finland a couple of weeks later that we did anything about our TV aerial and the upraised shed.

Our tall beech tree had withstood the force of the winds but when exceptional gales again swept the country the following year I noticed that the grass surrounding its trunk was literally heaving and felt that we could not take any more chances with it – who knows what might have happened if there had been a third time? So it had to be felled, to be later replaced by a flowering cherry which is itself quite a size now.

* * * * *

That visit to Finland was one of several. We liked the country and its people and we came to know Helsinki quite well. We were already familiar with Oslo, where we had also visited the Olympic ski jump at Holmenkollen, and other parts of southern Norway. Another favourite port of call was the Resistance Museum in the Akershaus, where one can see exhibits depicting the privations of the Norwegians during the war and the ingenuity of the underground movement in producing clandestine newspapers and constructing illicit radio sets during the years of German occupation.

On Audrey's last visit to Norway in 1998, Lars drove us into the mountains to the old power station at Rjukan, where in the war the Germans realised that it provided a source of the heavy water needed to make atomic bombs. They were only prevented from making use of it when Norwegian partisans, aided by British air attack and ground agents, put the power station out of action. A film has been made about this.

Audrey, Elizabeth and I also made a journey by train, coach and ship from Oslo to Fläm, and to Voss and on to Bergen, where we stayed the night before taking the train back through the mountains to Oslo. Believe me, the scenery is breathtaking.

In Finland we not only explored the capital but drove to the Russian border to see round a hunting lodge of the former Czars, and to the southern extremity of the country at Hango. On another occasion Lars and I took the ferry across the Gulf of Finland to Tallinn, the capital of Estonia, a Baltic country which had been under Russian domination but had gained its independence by the time we went.

Audrey and Lars at Rjukan

As well as these visits to Norway and Finland we found time to have caravan holidays in various places in England, Scotland and Wales, and, with Bunty and Arthur, to go to Spain, Malta, Portugal and Tenerife. Early in 1985 we made our longest journey – to Swaziland, way down in southern Africa where Peter was on the staff of the British High Commission in Mbabane.

The flight to Africa was via Madrid, where we changed planes in the middle of the night, and Peter met us at the airport in

Johannesburg for the long drive to Mbabane. At this time apartheid was still being strictly enforced in South Africa, and I remember how shocked Audrey and I were to see the way in which some whites treated, and addressed, the blacks. So much has changed, thank goodness, in the intervening years, as I have observed on visits to South Africa in 2001 and 2002.

During our stay in Swaziland we all went on a fascinating trip through Zululand. This took us to Rorke's Drift, where the small beleaguered British garrison held out against a much larger force of natives in the Zulu War of 1879 (Michael Caine starred in the film about this). We didn't quite make it to Isandhlwana, where thousands lost their lives in a fierce battle (Vivienne was expecting Annie at the time and couldn't take what would have been a very jolting ride along a rough track) but we did go on to Ulundi, where the final battle took place and where we visited the cemetery of the British war dead.

Rorke's Drift

Peter, Vivienne and Audrey, Emma and Jessica in Swaziland

* * * * *

At home we were always happy in Waldringfield. We had soon made many friends and, yet again, found that we had really exceptional neighbours in Kit and Joe Clark. People living in villages fall into one of three categories, I think. There are those who know everybody, who are a mine of information about what is going on and who play an active part in just about everything; then there are those who just live in the village and don't join in anything; finally, the third group consists of people who socialise in a minor way and support causes and activities but don't take on any particularly active role. Audrey and I fell into the last category, though I did for short time take on the duties of clerk to the Parochial Church Council. With Ken Green I took up golf and for five years we played regularly on the nine-hole course at Cretingham. Audrey and Ken's wife,

Freda, also became close companions, and we formed lasting friendships with others in the village. I would mention especially Bill and Alma Wells, Frank and Agnes Gross, Edward Stanley and Joy Savage. Sadly, I have to record that both Bill Wells and Ken Green have recently died, both in their eighties.

Christmas 1988 at Waldringfield
From top: Audrey, Elizabeth, Fredrik, Lars, Thomas and William

When our twelfth grandchild, Sophie, was born in Delhi in 1988 Audrey flew to India to be with Vivienne, Peter and the other three girls for a short visit – just two weeks – which did not allow her to do much, if any, sightseeing, though she couldn't avoid noticing the large number of beggars there were around.

In September 1990 we joined our life-long friends, Dorrie and Keith Wood, at a family luncheon in celebration of their 50th wedding anniversary. That very same afternoon Audrey kept an appointment at our doctor's, having earlier discovered a lump in her right breast. The doctor told her that she would almost certainly have to undergo a mastectomy, and arranged for her to be admitted a week later, on Tuesday 1st October. Audrey took this disturbing news very calmly. In fact, I'm sure that I displayed more anxiety than she did.

She duly went into Ipswich Hospital on the Tuesday and made a good recovery from the operation the next day. Over the following five years, during which she was taking the drug Tamoxifen, we visited the hospital at intervals for mammo-grams and other checks, getting the all clear every time. It was a blessing for both of us that, in 1995, we had no inkling that four years on Audrey would be a cancer victim for the second time. She was the third in our immediate family to have breast cancer: Bunty had a mastectomy in 1988 and Una in 1989. And so the years passed without any further problems for Audrey so far as the mastectomy was concerned. Apart from a swollen arm, which was not unusual, that also applied to Bunty, but Una developed secondary cancer, becoming much weaker as time went on.

It was about the time of Audrey's operation that Emma started as a boarder at Brandeston School, the junior part of Framling-ham College which she went on to a year or so later. Emma was followed at Brandeston and Framlingham by Jessica and Annie, so over a period of about ten years Audrey and I, as guardians of our grandchildren while their parents were overseas, had close associations with both schools, their heads and other staff, and we attended many functions. In September 2002 Sophie also started at Framlingham College while Annie became a boarder at Woodbridge School. I must say that during the years 2001-2003 I missed the contact with the girls' schools; now I have renewed it.

* * * * *

Audrey with Dixie at Culloden in June 1981…

... and painting the fence at The Paddocks in 1991

Several times during the '80s Audrey and I kept house for Stephen and Dot at their home in Warwickshire while they were abroad at travel conferences. One of our (enjoyable) tasks was to ferry Jenalynn and Tracy to and from gymnastic sessions at Warwick University, the swimming pool in Coventry and the homes of their various friends, and I shall never forget a particular night when Stephen and Dot were away in Canada.

Audrey was in the house with Jenalynn, who was doing her homework, and Charlotte, while I had taken my car out to fetch Tracy from a friend's. On our return I was met by an anxious Audrey who told me that, on taking Charlotte upstairs to see her into bed, she had found that the door to the main bedroom (Steve's and Dot's) would not open – it was obviously locked from the inside.

It was then that I saw the open window at the front end of the bedroom. So, getting a ladder from the garage, I climbed up with a torch and shone the light into the room. I could hardly believe my eyes: the room was in complete disorder, with possessions strewn all over the bed.

"We've been burgled," I called out to Audrey and the girls, waiting at the bottom of the ladder. And with that I was about to climb through the window to investigate when, realising that discretion is the better part of valour and fearing that an intruder might be waiting for me with a weapon, I hurriedly descended to the ground and dialled '999' for the police. Very soon a police car with investigating officers was on the scene – but by then the intruder had escaped. It appeared that he had got in by forcing the front window and departed through a window at the other end of the room, where there was a balcony – probably as soon as he heard Audrey trying to open the door. The contents of Stephen's briefcase were later found scattered on the ground in a field behind the house, but the burglar got away with £8,000 worth of jewellery.

The very next day Stephen and Dot returned from their visit to Canada. Stephen quite thought I was joking when I told him that the house had been burgled, but as I had left the bedroom just as it was with everything strewn about, he soon realised that I was serious.

Some time later a Liverpool man was on trial for other offences and admitted the break-in, asking for it to be taken into consideration before he was sentenced. Quite an experience for us!

In 1988 Stephen, who had obtained his pilot's licence and acquired his own light aircraft, made three flights from Coventry to Suffolk, each time landing at Ipswich Airport – now the site of a large housing estate. There was a dramatic ending to the second of these flights, with Charlotte as a passenger: he lost his way towards its end and landed near Colchester at what turned out to be a disused airfield which was being used by the military. Very quickly someone appeared from a hut, told Stephen where he was and directed him towards Ipswich. Meanwhile, with IRA terrorist activity on everyone's mind at the time and a military presence in the area, the police at Ipswich were alerted. So on finally landing at the airport Stephen was met by CID officers, who interrogated him in one room and Charlotte in another, while Audrey and I waited anxiously outside. It all ended happily when Stephen emerged to tell us that he had been able to satisfy the police that neither he nor Charlotte had any connection whatsoever with any terrorist activity. I think we must give full marks for security alertness.

On his first visit by air Stephen took me for a thrilling flight over the Orwell Bridge and Felixstowe, where I was able to spot our old house, then up the Deben and over Waldringfield. On the third of these flights he brought with him a microwave oven as a Christmas present to us. It amuses me to tell visitors that it was delivered by air!

In May 1988 Stephen, Andrew and I went to the Normandy battlefields. This was my second visit since 1944 but for my sons it was their first, and I know they found it a memorable experience to be guided by me to the beach where I landed just after D–Day, through the bocage country to the villages where our tanks had been in action and to the war museum at Bayeux. But even before we drove off the ferry at Ouisterham, the port for Caen, there was an incident worth recording. Andrew and I, driving down to Portsmouth from Waldringfield at night, had arranged to meet Stephen at the dockside early in the morning. As sailing time approached, however, there was no sign of Stephen at all. Then, at almost the last minute, he arrived from Warwickshire with a badly cracked windscreen. It appeared that he had overslept, had pushed his *BMW* almost to its limit to reach us in time and, to make matters worse, had hit a large bird – hence the damaged screen. Although the car was driveable it was a few days before we could get a new windscreen fitted in France.

For Andrew, it was just a weekend in Normandy as he had to return home in time to go back to work on the Monday. But we did make the most of the few days that the three of us were together – not in the least when I introduced my sons to the delights of Calvados, the very potent spirit of Normandy!

After seeing Andrew off on the ferry, Stephen and I continued for the rest of the week on a journey following much the same route that Audrey and I had taken in the *Capri* three years earlier. But this time we went on from Hamburg to the 'end of the line' – Berlin. Since I had left that city in 1946 virtually all traces of war damage had disappeared, though what had been left of a famous church in the centre still stood almost as it was 42 years before, and a new structure had appeared on the scene – the Berlin Wall (to be demolished a year or so later with the reunification of East and West Germany). Stephen and I were able to mount a viewing platform to see what lay on the other side of the wall – a bleak open space at the end of which stood the equally bleak buildings of East Berlin.

We went, too, to the Olympic Stadium, scene of the 1936 Games, where Hitler used to address rallies of thousands of Nazis before the war. In fact, I got Stephen to stand on what we were convinced was the exact spot where the late, but not lamented, Führer himself stood to deliver his addresses.

At Mundesley in 1989 with our friends Ken and Freda Green

*Dot, Jenalynn, Stephen, Tracy and Charlotte
with two of their dogs*

With the dawn of 1992 Audrey and I were approaching the day when we would celebrate our Golden Wedding. It didn't seem possible that half a century had passed since we walked down the aisle at the church in Stowmarket in March 1942, yet in that time we had produced a family which had become twenty strong. We marked the occasion with a party at home and shortly afterwards enjoyed the present our children gave us: two days in London, staying at a four star hotel in Grosvenor Square near the United States Embassy, and seats at the *Albert Hall* for one of the last concerts Frank Sinatra gave in Britain.

This surprise was a particular delight for Audrey as she had been a great admirer of Sinatra for many years – since, in fact, our days at Sutton Coldfield when our near neighbour Joyce Crowe had us round in the evenings to listen to his records. Despite his years – he was 76 – Sinatra was in great form, though he did have an autocue so he wouldn't be lost for words. On the programme, too, were Humphrey Lyttleton and his wife Cleo Laine, and Sinatra's backing orchestra was conducted by his son. After this truly exciting evening Audrey and I walked back to our hotel along the fringe of Kensington Gardens.

It was Normandy again for me and Audrey in June 1994 when we revisited the beaches with Greta and Dennis. As a former paratrooper Dennis was, of course, particularly interested when we went to Pegasus Bridge, seized by British paras and glider troops 50 years earlier. Driving along the coast on another day to a beach where landings had taken place, we found ourselves beside a group of young English servicemen and women gathered in a circle for a talk about the D-Day operation being given by an experienced military guide. Dennis and I were able to add a bit of unexpected colour to the occasion when we revealed that we had both been involved in the 1944 invasion of the continent and that I had actually taken part in the Normandy landing. Modern warfare aside, the four of us also took the opportunity to see the famous Bayeux Tapestry which, I suppose, must be the longest in the world.

Sharing a joke on the beach at Felixstowe

Our Golden Wedding anniversary in March 1992

Since the summer of 1996 Vivienne and Peter have had a home in Waldringfield – a bungalow in Sunnyhill just a few minutes' walk away from *The Old School House*. Returning to England that year after four years in Australia, and having sold their house in Surrey, they needed a new home base before departing for their next posting in Cameroon. It has been, of course, a bonus for us to have them so close when in England.

On 23rd September 1996 I celebrated my 80th birthday little knowing, or even suspecting, beforehand what my children had organised to mark this event.

There were two surprises: the first was a lunch at *Rules*, London's oldest restaurant, and on the day Audrey and I set off from home thinking that at the restaurant we would be joined just by Stephen who was giving the lunch for us.

Tony's 80th Birthday Luncheon

Venue

Rules

London's Oldest Resturant

35 Maiden Lane

Covent Garden

London WC2

Tel: 0171 836 5314

Time 12.30 - 1.00 p.m.   *Monday 23rd Sept 1996*

On our arrival, to our surprise we were shown to a table set for five – and there was no Stephen. The mystery was solved after a few minutes when my sisters Bunty and Una, with Arthur, suddenly appeared to join us at the table. And Stephen? He let us enjoy the meal and celebrate on our own, joining us for a few minutes towards the end, having taken a short time off from his work in the city.

Surprise number two came a few days later. Elizabeth, Lars and their boys were staying with us and on the Sunday we left the house to have a pub lunch – or so I thought. Lars drove us to the *Marlborough Hotel* in Ipswich. For a pub lunch? No reply from Lars to that question. On arriving at the hotel Audrey and I were directed to go through a door opening from the foyer. To my complete astonishment I found myself facing my entire family gathered round the tables set for lunch – all 21 of them! Who could wish for a more appropriate and splendid birthday gift from their children? My heartfelt thanks went to all of them, especially to Stephen and Andrew for organising this gathering of the clan.

Our thirteen grandchildren at the Marlborough Hotel

The whole family

Several months elapsed before I was able to enjoy my special '80th' present – a flight in a Richard Branson hot-air balloon. This was an unforgettable experience and one which I would recommend to anyone who is hale and hearty. I suppose there is really nothing quite like such a flight, except perhaps to go up in a glider; gently floating along a thousand or so feet above the ground, the silence is such a contrast to the noise one experiences in an aeroplane flight – except, of course, when the blower is switched on to send a sheet of flame to heat the air inside the balloon.

We took off from a field south of Framlingham, the watching figures of Audrey, Anne and Henry quickly shrinking to doll-like proportions as we rose into the sky. As we floated northwards over Brandeston, Framlingham Castle and the college where my granddaughters were at school, the three of them, in Anne and Henry's car, followed my progress. I think that, having to stick to the roads whereas the balloon was able to soar over fields, farms and houses, they lost sight of us towards the end of the flight, missing out on the actual moment of our eventual landing. But they caught up with us and joined me, and the others who had been in the basket, when as darkness was beginning to fall we enjoyed glasses of champagne after taking part in the operation to pack the balloon and other equipment, which was then loaded on to Land Rovers. On that single hour-long flight I saw, and took in, more of the Suffolk countryside than I'd been able to before, or will ever do.

By March 1999 Audrey and I had notched up 57 years of marriage, and in May of that year we had a holiday on the island of Alderney. It was to prove our last together. We had chosen Alderney on the recommendation of Emma and her boyfriend, Adam, who had earlier been camping there, and a very good choice it turned out to be. Alderney is a delightful, unspoilt island with historic and World War II associations, walks and forts – and no unwanted amusements. We walked every day, covering the island from one end to the other.

It was a wonderfully happy holiday and I think the only thing that Audrey didn't like about it was the method of getting there and back from the mainland. That was by air in a very small plane seating about ten people. We sat side by side, there being no gangway, each of us beside a window, so Audrey's wish not to have a window seat just couldn't be fulfilled.

* * * * *

From about the mid-'80s to the present day I have from time to time had renewed contacts with the Royal Tank Regiment. Twice, at Thame in Oxfordshire, I was among a small group of former members of the Wireless Wing at the pre-OCTU at Blackdown who met to reminisce about our days together during the war. My long-time friend, Chris Gray, whom I have met several times over the years, was there, as was the actor

Raymond Francis, whose real name was Thompson. Our evenings at the hotel in Thame were spirited in more ways than one!

On two occasions I went to London to attend memorial services. One was for Lieutenant-Colonel Pat Hobart, my commanding officer in 1 RTR from the Normandy beach-head to Berlin. Tragically, he and his wife had both been killed in a car accident. At the service, for the first time since the early days of the Normandy campaign I met the man who had appointed me Signals Officer of the regiment in 1944, and who had risen to the highest rank in the British Army – Field-Marshall Lord Carver.

The other memorial service, to which Audrey came with me, was for Raymond Francis. After the service we joined the many show business people who attended a reception at the Garrick Club, where we met Ray's son, the actor Clive Francis.

In November 1998 I went to London again, on the Sunday after Remembrance Day, to take part in a Royal Tank Regiment march past the Cenotaph in Whitehall. Emma, then engaged in her nursing training, had met me beforehand and was able to find a good position on the route to take photographs.

I've been jumping ahead with these recollections, and I could quite easily have got the sequence wrong. Not that that really matters though, and while writing of matters military I might as well mention other events which will take us up to 2002.

In the summer of 2000 Lord Carver came to East Anglia to unveil a memorial to the 7th Armoured Division in the shape of a restored *Cromwell* tank. This memorial, a permanent fixture, is set in Thetford forest near to the area where I was with 1 RTR in the days leading up to D-Day in June 1944.

It was my misfortune to be out of the country when the unveiling took place, and I was in Cape Town early in

December 2001 when I learnt of Lord Carver's sudden death at the age of 86. Fortunately, I was back at home in time to attend a memorial service to this famous soldier at Winchester Cathedral. There was a congregation of several hundred people from many walks of life, not the least, of course, from the Armed Services. The Queen and the Prime Minister were both represented, and the Royal Tank Regiment Band played.

Much nearer home I have been to two RTR events at Orwell Park School, near Ipswich. My readers may remember that in 1944 it was in the grounds of Orwell Park, sloping down to the river, that 1 RTR and other units of the 22nd Armoured Brigade of the 7th Armoured Division waterproofed their vehicles, tracked and wheeled, in readiness for the landings in France.

The first gathering in 2001 was a reunion which brought together surviving veterans of the regiments which took part in the Normandy operation, and the highlight of this occasion was the unveiling of a commemorative plaque to the 7th Armoured Division in the school grounds. A wartime *Sherman* tank, brought up from Kent, created much interest as did another tank, again from Kent, which was displayed on the occasion of the second such reunion at Orwell Park a year later, in September 2002. For both these events, those of us who enjoyed the opportunity to meet old comrades and were very generously entertained are greatly indebted to Orwell Park School and its headmaster, Mr Andrew Auster. A third reunion was fixed for September 2003.

So East Anglia in general, and Suffolk in particular, will always have good reason to remember the presence of the famous Desert Rats in their midst during the days when victory in Europe was almost within the grasp of the Allies in World War II.

The memorial plaque to the Desert Rats in Orwell Park

**Memorial to the Royal Tank Regiment
unveiled by the Queen in 2000**

I have the happiest memories of the innumerable occasions when Audrey and I, sometimes on our own or perhaps with Anne and Henry, at others with our children and grandchildren, enjoyed outings and picnics in the Suffolk countryside and especially on the beaches at Felixstowe – the one at the bottom of Jacob's Ladder comes to mind – when we'd all go swimming. On one such occasion, visiting Southwold with the family, we left our car on an open-ground carpark near the shopping area, and on returning to it later in the day for the homeward journey we failed to ensure that our little dog was safely in the car before we drove off. It wasn't until we were well clear of the town that we suddenly realised that Dixie wasn't with us. So there was a hurried turn round and we sped back to the parking area to find Dixie patiently waiting for us just where we'd left her – great sighs of relief!

A favourite place for both of us was Dunwich Heath, with its former coastguard cottages, National Trust shop and café, walks across the heath-covered headland and along the beach stretching one way to Walberswick and the other to the atomic power station at Sizewell, and the bird sanctuary and nature reserve at Minsmere close by. These were particularly happy days, and it is to Dunwich Heath that I now go on my own to reflect on the times when Audrey was with me there.

In 1994 Lucy was born in Brisbane, and the tail-end of the '90s and early part of the new millennium saw the first weddings among our grandchildren: Jenalynn was married to Richard Ancliff in June 1997 at Honiley Church, near Warwick. Unfortunately, it was a rainy day; nevertheless, it was a most enjoyable occasion for a large gathering of family and friends. Four years later, in May 2001, Victoria and Johnny McAteer were married in the Parish Church at Woolpit, Suffolk; this time the sun shone brilliantly and again there was a large assembly of family and friends.

After Lucy's christening at Waldringfield in 1996

With our friend Audrey Butler

With Una (left) and Bunty (right) at Newlands Corner in 1998

The Saddest Time of My Life

1999-2000 – and beyond

I now come to a painful chapter of our lives for it covers the period from the autumn of 1999, when Audrey was taken ill, to the day of her death in May 2000.

In August 1999 we spent a few days in Norfolk with our good friend, Audrey Butler, with whom we had exchanged many visits over the years. Audrey didn't seem to be quite as well as usual, though there wasn't anything that one could put one's finger on. But not long after our return home we knew that something was seriously wrong and on 24th August I took her to our doctor's. The lady doctor, deputising for Audrey's, who examined her decided that she would have to be seen by a gynaecologist.

On 31st August we both attended the funeral of Audrey's cousin by marriage, Peggy Thurgood. Audrey was not at all well that day and we came home as soon as possible. In the early hours of the next day, 1st September, I had to summon the emergency call doctor, who came at 5.00 am. Later that morning Audrey was seen by our own doctor, who arranged for her to be admitted to Ipswich Hospital right away. By 11.15 am she was in a hospital bed and being examined by the consultant doctor. He broke the bad news that she had a growth in the uterus which he would remove in the course of carrying out a hysterectomy.

The operation took place on Saturday, 4th September, and to my great relief her recovery followed a normal course – there were no complications. But that was short-lived. The doctor explained that while he had removed the main cancerous growth, Audrey would have to have chemotherapy treatment and he could not say how effective that would be. Audrey accepted the verdict with the great calmness that she always showed; to me, the news was devastating but I knew that I would have to face up to the days that lay ahead. And, ever an optimist, I tried to convince myself that, in the fullness of time, Audrey's good health would be restored.

Various family members and friends were frequent visitors to the hospital during the two weeks she was a patient. Among them was Vivienne, who with Lucy had been at home in the village (from Cameroon) since early June, but she had to fly back to Cameroon on 11th September. Two days later Elizabeth arrived from Norway and on the 13th we brought Audrey home.

With Audrey home again I set about taking on the dual roles of cook-housekeeper and nurse (not, of course, in the latter role taking on the tasks so well carried out by the helpful and efficient district nurses who came to the house regularly). And there were not only frequent day visits to the hospital but times when Audrey had to stay in as a patient. The chemotherapy treatments were extremely weakening and after three of the six that had been scheduled the consultant stopped them, deciding that Audrey couldn't take any more. That was not surprising for when her blood count became very low she had to be given transfusions, and on two occasions when she collapsed I had to dial '999' for an ambulance in the middle of the night, each time calling on our ever-helpful neighbour Kit Clark for the wonderful support which I knew she would always give, and did.

There were times when Audrey seemed to be getting a little better. Then we would drive to Felixstowe where she would take short walks on the Prom, or to a small picnic spot at Melton where there were ducks on the pond. Our longest trip was to Andrew's at Beyton; we had hoped that Audrey would be strong enough to make the car journey to Stephen's, but that was not to be. As time went on, in 2000, the short walks tended to be confined to the garden.

During most days Audrey was able to rest in the living room and I made her as comfortable as possible on a new large settee which Stephen and I bought. There were visitors, of course, both family and friends. No-one could have been more caring or thoughtful than Anne, whose practical help with many meals was invaluable. Marjorie, so much older and less active, made her contribution by insisting on buying us a new washing machine when our old one came to the end of its life – and flooded the kitchen. Yes, one morning I went into the kitchen to be confronted by a rising pool of water, and yet again our neighbours came to the rescue. Joe mopped up the water and when we had got the sopping wet washing out of the machine Kit not only got it dry but ironed it all.

It was fortunate that Vivienne, Peter and their girls were at home in the village for the Christmas of 1999. I was excused cooking duties on Christmas day, Vivienne bringing the meal to us. This was to be Audrey's last Christmas, though I tried to convince myself, and Audrey, that as time went on she would gain sufficient strength and be well enough to make the journey to Cape Town, Peter's next posting, which she knew he would be taking up in the coming summer. That, sadly, was not to happen. But we did manage to get Audrey to Vivienne's in Sunnyhill on 31st December to see in the new millennium.

Into the year 2000 our routine continued to follow its set course. There were ups and downs in Audrey's condition, but more of the latter as she became weaker. Hospital visits showed me that I had to accept the heart-breaking prospect that she was not going to recover. Throughout all the days and nights, and weeks, as she lay quietly with her own, unexpressed, thoughts she never once complained about anything. She bore her illness with great bravery, yet knowing, I'm sure in my own mind, what it was leading to very soon.

Audrey's 77th birthday with Anne (left) and Victoria (right)

At Waldringfield in summer 1999
with Elizabeth and Vivienne and their families

By 25th April she was admitted to hospital again and the next day she had two blood transfusions. That same day Vivienne arrived from Cameroon and three days later Elizabeth was here from Norway. On 1st May we brought Audrey home and on the 5th she just managed to walk to our summer house and back. But the next day, as her condition worsened, I had to call the emergency doctor and she was taken back into hospital by ambulance. On the 11th she was allowed to come home – again in an ambulance.

Over all this anxious period our four children were with us frequently – Stephen from Warwickshire, Andrew from West Suffolk and, as I have mentioned, Elizabeth and Vivienne.

By the weekend of Saturday-Sunday, 13th-14th May, when not only our children but our grandchildren and members of Audrey's own family came to her bedside, Audrey's condition had deteriorated. Elizabeth, Vivienne and I were with her into the night, and on the morning of Monday 15th May, she closed her eyes for the last time. It was 12.25 am.

My heartbreak at losing someone I had loved so dearly for almost sixty years has, from that moment onwards, been alleviated as far as possible by the tremendous support that I have received from my sons and daughters – four loving, caring and understanding people, themselves anguished by the loss of a devoted mother. There are times when I am alone in a physical sense – but not spiritually – and others, some quite long periods, when I am with one or other of them either in their own homes or mine. And my friends in Waldringfield and elsewhere, as well as other members of Audrey's wider family and mine, have been of tremendous help to me over the past three years.

I have to thank our Rector, the Rev John Waller, for allocating the fine spot in the extended churchyard at Waldringfield where Audrey is buried. It is just in front of a tall tree beneath which is a seat with a view of the River Deben across the fields. There are always flowers on her grave, and when I am away from home my caring sister-in-law, Anne, sees to it that the vases are replenished.

I'm sometimes asked how I am getting on and whether "…it gets any better" as time passes, and I like to quote the words of the late Elizabeth the Queen Mother, a widow for fifty years, when a similar question was put to her. She said, "No, it doesn't get any better but I'm getting better at it." I can say the same.

Audrey was one of eight children. There are three left now: Greta in Canada, Bernard at Stowupland and the youngest, Anne, in Ipswich. The eldest, Brenda, died in 1983, Jack in 1993, Kaye in 1998 and Marjorie eight months after Audrey in 2001. My younger sister, Una, died in 2001; Bunty and her husband Arthur are still in the house in Guildford which has been their home for sixty years.

I had seen Una in a nursing home just before I left for Cape Town on 28th January 2001. On the day of her funeral, a week after her death on 7th March, Vivienne and I went by arrangement to the South African Church of the Good Shepherd, which had been specially opened for us, at the time when the cremation service was taking place in England.

* * * * *

Since the loss of Audrey, a dear partner who is always in my thoughts and can never be replaced, I have become quite a traveller. So much so that I'm sure people in the village are quite surprised when they find me at home! I have been to Canada with Stephen and family, to Elizabeth's in Norway five times, to Vivienne's in Cape Town three times, to Stephen's in Warwickshire and Andrew's at Beyton and Bury St Edmunds, and to my sister's in Guildford, as well as spending a few days in France.

While in Cape Town I went to the top of the famous Table Mountain and to the Cape of Good Hope, the southernmost tip of Africa where it is commonly accepted that the Atlantic and Indian Oceans meet (actually they meet a little to the east). I paid several visits to the Kirstenbosch Botanical Garden – a truly marvellous place – and a particularly memorable experience was to take the boat to Robben Island, where Nelson Mandela spent most of his 27 years in prison. But my most abiding memory of my visits to Cape Town will be of Table Mountain and sitting on the terrace of Vivienne's house in the sunshine, having a meal or reading – or writing part of this book – and looking up at the spectacular massif so close to us.

In Norway, a country I have come to know well, I went with Elizabeth on an exhilarating journey from Oslo to the west coast, and back. We took the train north to Dombås, then went in another train to Åndalsnes and from there by coach to Ålesund, where, at midnight, we joined a cruise ship for a 14-hour voyage to Bergen, returning to the Oslo area by train. It was a fairytale journey through the mountains and along the fjords.

During an earlier visit to Norway, I think in 2001, Elizabeth and I revisited the Olympic ski jump. A lift took us part of the way up, and I then insisted on climbing on my own up a steep stairway (almost a ladder) to the very top – much to Elizabeth's indignation and displeasure. Quite understandably, she was worried for me and I realised afterwards that at my age it had been unfair to her to be so foolish.

Early in November 2002 I went with Stephen to a village in Gloucestershire to attend a lunch to commemorate the Diamond Wedding of my old friend, John Mumford, and his wife, Doreen. It will be remembered that John had brought Audrey and me together during the war, and this occasion was only the second time in 61 years that we had met. Not long afterwards I learnt that Harry Holt, my colleague on the *Star* from 1946 to 1953 and friend ever since those early post-war days, had been taken seriously ill at his home in Olton, Solihull, and moved to a hospital in Sussex to be near his daughter, Jennifer. A few weeks later I was grieved to learn of his death at the age of 86. His wife, Doreen, had died a month or so before Audrey in 2000.

I have been writing in December 2002, with Christmas fast approaching and preparations in hand for a big family gathering in Waldringfield. Now it is January 2003 – Christmas has come and gone and we are in a new year. With the exception of Stephen, Dot and their three girls, and my two baby great-granddaughters, Elliemay and Katie, who celebrated in Warwickshire, and Andrew's two daughters, in West Suffolk, everyone in the family was here with me for all, or part, of the Yuletide festivities. Elizabeth and Lars, with Fredrik, Thomas and William, arrived in good time from snow-covered Norway, followed by Vivienne, Annie, Sophie and Lucy from Cape Town (then destined for Peter's new posting to San Francisco in February), Emma coming from London and Jessica and her boyfriend, Vincenzo, from Cambridge, and, on Christmas Eve, Andrew and Pat for a family party at Vivienne's.

It was a wonderful Christmas when fourteen of us sat down for dinner round two tables in *The Old School House*. On Christmas Eve, Emma, Jessica and Annie had accompanied me to Midnight Mass in the village church. But for me, especially, and for my children there was sadness that Audrey was not with us to enjoy this exceptional reunion, and my mind went back three years to her last Christmas, and to her seeing in the new Millennium, with Vivienne and her family.

Audrey and myself in Norway in 1998

On the patio of Vivienne's house in Cape Town

Epilogue

I think I have now reached the point where I should bring this account of my life, thus far, to a close. In all honesty I can say that it has been a very good life in every way. I look back on a happy childhood, despite family ups and downs and the loss of my mother when I was only 3 (compensated for by the love and care I received from my step-mother over many years); on schooldays of which I also have happy memories; on war days from which I was fortunate to emerge unscathed; on 58 years of the happiest marriage anyone could wish for; on over 24 years of enjoyable and active retirement; on the upbringing and successful marriages of two sons and two daughters; and on the growth of my family to a total of 13 grandchildren and, just recently, the arrival of two great-granddaughters.

Who could ask for more? I have been a most fortunate man, thankful as anyone could be for the many blessings bestowed on me. And these continue – my children and my grandchildren all show me the greatest love and care.

During my long life the world has been changing at an ever-increasing rate. Yet some things never seem to change: we were at war when I was born and now, in the spring of 2003, we are again involved in a war, this time with Saddam Hussein's Iraq. I had hoped, as so many millions of people worldwide had hoped, that armed conflict would be avoided, but it was not to be.

Meanwhile, within the family, Peter, Vivienne and Lucy have gone off to San Francisco, where Peter has started a four-year posting as the British Consul there. Emma, living in London with her boy-friend, Adam Edwards, is a nurse in the children's intensive care ward at Guy's Hospital, having gained a nursing diploma at university, and is now expecting to take a degree course. Jessica and *her* boy-friend, Vincenzo Giovanniello, are both in Cambridge; Jess gained an Art and Design Diploma and is seeking a post in Graphic Design. Vincenzo is studying British History and Politics at Anglia Polytechnic University. Annie and Sophie are both boarders in Suffolk – Annie at Woodbridge School preparing for her A-levels and Sophie at Framlingham College, where she will be taking her GCSEs in 2004. Lucy is at school in Mill Valley, California.

Elizabeth's Thomas is an accomplished musician, and after doing his National Service in Norway he came to England where he immersed himself in IT/Media Studies at London University; Fredrik, also very musical, is working in Oslo, and William is attending a music school not far from home in Billingstad.

All three of Stephen's daughters gained university degrees. Jenalynn, Richard and their one-year-old daughter, Elliemay Audrey, have a house in Kenilworth, Jen continuing her work as an IT projects manager. Tracy, who is in corporate marketing with British Airways in New York, returned to England in September, with baby Katie Elizabeth, for her marriage to Stephen Harrison, also with BA, and Charlotte and her partner, Mark Billyeald, have a flat in Kenilworth. Like Mark, a teacher, Charlotte has this year forsaken the schoolroom to take over the running of a livery at Stephen's farm in the village of Beausale, near Warwick. Stephen himself has retired.

Andrew's girls are both in Suffolk, Victoria having settled in the village of Woolpit, where she and Johnny McAteer were married, and Sarah in nearby Thurston with her partner, Johnny Rookard. Victoria is PA to a director of a firm of accountants while Sarah has been a nursery nurse for several years. Sarah and Johnny have just become engaged – so another wedding is on the horizon.

Thomas on National Service

Emma with her mother after her graduation at the Royal Festival Hall in 2000

Andrew and Pat with Victoria and Sarah

And thus the family continues to grow, spreading its wings far and wide!

Au revoir!

Waldringfield, September 2003